Henry Fawcett

Free Trade And Protection

Henry Fawcett

Free Trade And Protection

ISBN/EAN: 9783744725910

Printed in Europe, USA, Canada, Australia, Japan

Cover: Foto ©ninafisch / pixelio.de

More available books at **www.hansebooks.com**

FREE TRADE

AND

PROTECTION

BY THE

RIGHT HON. HENRY FAWCETT, M.P., D.C.L., F.R.S.,

FELLOW OF TRINITY HALL,

AND PROFESSOR OF POLITICAL ECONOMY IN THE UNIVERSITY OF CAMBRIDGE.

SIXTH EDITION.

𝔏𝔬𝔫𝔡𝔬𝔫:

MACMILLAN AND CO.

1885.

TABLE OF CONTENTS.

PREFACE TO THE SIXTH EDITION.

THIS sixth edition of *Free Trade and Protection* is necessarily little more than a reprint of the fifth edition, the last revised by my husband himself. I have, however, carried out what I believe would have been his wishes, and have, with very few exceptions, brought all the statistical facts and illustrations up to the present date. In doing this I have received valuable assistance from Mr. F. J. Dryhurst, who from 1871 till 1884 was my husband's able and devoted secretary; also from Sir Thomas Farrer and Mr. R. Giffen of the Board of Trade. I wish to take this opportunity of acknowledging the help so readily afforded me by them, and of thanking them sincerely for it. I have also obtained a great many facts and figures from the *Statistical Abstracts* issued annually by the Board of Trade, and from the

Statesman's Year Book published by Messrs. Macmillan and Co.

I have in a few cases inserted notes; but as these are signed with my initials they can be readily distinguished from the original text.

MILLICENT GARRETT FAWCETT.

February, 1885.

PREFACE TO THE FIFTH EDITION.

As only a few months have passed since the fourth edition of this book was published, I think it unnecessary to introduce any alterations into the present edition. At the time when the chapter on commercial treaties was written, it was still doubtful whether the Anglo-French commercial treaty, which was on the point of expiring, would be renewed. All hope of such a renewal is now at any rate for a time relinquished. As in this chapter I have considered the disadvantages as well as the advantages of commercial treaties, it is, I think, better to let the chapter stand as it was originally written.

Within the last few weeks definite action has been taken upon another subject which is referred to in the following pages. Nearly all the Indian import duties, including those on cotton goods, are about to be repealed. The objections which I have always thought might be urged against the repeal of the Indian cotton duties, if it had been necessary to replace the revenue they yielded by fresh taxation, do not apply when, in consequence of a

marked improvement in Indian finance, the loss of revenue
can not only be supplied without any fresh burden being
imposed upon the tax-payers, but the surplus is sufficient to
enable the repeal of the cotton duties to be accompanied
by other important remissions of taxation.

March, 1882.

PREFACE TO THE FOURTH EDITION.

THE advantages conferred upon England by Free Trade have been so striking that for a long time we were too much in the habit of ignoring the strong position occupied by Protection on the Continent, in the United States and in many of our Colonies. Although I believe it can be shown that nothing has occurred either to make us estimate these advantages less highly than we have formerly done, or to encourage any departure from the principles of Free Trade, yet I am afraid it cannot be denied that within the last few years not only has Protection gained strength in Protectionist countries, but even in England itself there is a certain reaction against Free Trade. It therefore seems to me to become the more important carefully to consider the causes which have given the principles of Protection their present vitality. Although there may probably be no fear that Protection will again be introduced into England, yet a re-statement of the principles of Free Trade cannot be out of place when it is observed that even in England many of those who profess strong adherence to these principles hold them by so slender a thread that when they settle in our Colonies, and are surrounded by a somewhat different set of economic circumstances, they become in numerous instances ardent protectionists.

Although I have not thought it necessary in this edition to alter the general arrangement of the book, yet some parts of it have been re-written, with the object of connecting it as far as possible with the phases of the protectionist and free-trade movements which are now assuming most practical importance.

I again wish to express my thanks to my wife, and to my secretary, Mr. F. J. Dryhurst, for the aid they have rendered me in preparing this edition for the press.

November, 1881.

PREFACE TO THE FIRST EDITION.

In the autumn of last year I delivered at Cambridge a course of Lectures on Free Trade and Protection. One of the chief objects I had in view was to endeavour to explain the causes which have retarded the progress of Free Trade, and which have enabled Protectionists still to occupy so strong a position on the Continent, in America, and in many of our Colonies. I first thought of publishing these Lectures almost in the form in which they were delivered; but I afterwards came to the conclusion that it would be better, for many reasons, to adopt a different arrangement, and I have consequently divided the book into six chapters.

I have had occasion frequently to refer to Mr. Frederick Martin's *Statesman's Year Book*, and I have also derived great assistance from the admirably-arranged *Statistical Abstracts* which are published annually by the Board of Trade. Whenever I have required additional information bearing on the subjects to which these Abstracts refer it has always been most readily supplied to me by two gentlemen holding official positions at the Board of Trade —Mr. Edwin J. Pearson, and Mr. Robert Giffen, the well-known economist and statist. I desire here to acknowledge their kindness, and to offer them my sincere thanks.

I also wish to say how much I appreciate the assistance I have derived from my wife, who has revised the book as it was passing through the press, and from my secretary, Mr. F. J. Dryhurst, who has not only acted as my amanuensis, but who has constantly aided me in various ways, and has prepared a summary of contents, which I believe will prove useful for purposes of reference.

May, 1878.

SUMMARY OF CONTENTS.

CHAPTER I.

INTRODUCTORY REMARKS.

THE extension of protection in Europe, the United States, and
many of the English Colonies in recent years.—The expectations, formerly entertained in this country, that the
example of England in adopting a free-trade policy would be
followed by other nations, have not been realized.—Nothing
is more likely to retard the cause of free trade than to underrate the strength of the opposition to it, and to ignore the
arguments of its opponents.—The adoption of free trade in
England was hastened by the fact that protection was most
strictly carried out with regard to agriculture, and consequently its most obvious result was the rise in the price of
food ; while, in other countries, protection is almost entirely
confined to manufactured products.—The abolition of protection may cause much suffering and loss to those employed
in the industries which have been brought into existence
through protection.—This loss corresponds to that which is
caused to workmen who possess special manual skill in any
handicraft, if the necessity for their labour is superseded
by the invention of a machine.—The motives which have
prompted the opposition to the introduction of free trade in
America and other countries are analogous to those which
have led workmen employed in certain trades to resist the
introduction of machinery.—The adoption of protectionist
principles in the Colonies has been encouraged by the opinion
expressed by Mr. Mill, that the imposition of a protective
duty, with the view of promoting a new industry in a recently-

CHAPTER II.

PROTECTION.

PART I.—*Bounties on Exports and Protective Subsidies.*

Protection has been in recent times supported with the object
of giving assistance to home industry, and has been chiefly
carried out by giving bounties on exports and imposing restraints on imports.—The system of encouraging exports and
discouraging imports was a product of the mercantile system,
and was originally adopted with the object of securing a
"favourable balance of trade."—Protection is now chiefly
carried out by imposing import duties; bounties on exports
are, however, occasionally granted at the present time.—
Formerly bounties on exports were as general in England
as protective duties on imports. The effect of the bounties
on the export, and restraints on the import, of corn which
formerly prevailed in England.—Examination of the effects
produced by the bounty given on the export of sugar from
France.—This bounty simply enables the English people, and
others who use French sugar, to purchase it at considerably
below cost price; the reduction in price approximating to the
amount of the bounty.—The only class who can permanently
profit from any particular produce being made artificially dear
are the owners of the land on which the produce is grown.—
Reasons against the proposal of the English sugar refiners that

they should be protected against French competition by the imposition of an import duty equivalent to the amount of the bounty.—The principles involved in the system of giving bounties on shipping may be considered in connection with the shipping bounties lately introduced in France.—These bounties or subsidies take the form of certain payments to shipbuilders according to the tonnage built, and to shipowners according to the number of miles run.—The object of the bounty on shipbuilding is stated to be to "compensate shipbuilders for the charges fixed by the Custom House tariff," and· its advocates urge that it involves no interference with the principles of free trade because foreign ships are still freely admitted to French ports.—In discussing the consequences of carrying out this form of protection, it is necessary to consider its effects upon those who enjoy the protection, and also upon those who provide the funds from which the protection is given.—Dealing first with the latter, it appears that the money can be supplied from no other source than the general taxation of the country, and therefore the whole community is taxed for the benefit of a special class.—If the principle is conceded of devoting public money to compensate a particular industry for the injury inflicted on it by protective import duties, other industries can put forward cogent claims to receive similar compensation.—Secondly, the effect on the shipbuilders who receive the subsidies will be not to give them higher profits and wages, but to reduce the price at which they can sell their ships.—The position which French shipping is expected to occupy after these bounties have been in operation contrasted with the position of English shipping, the progress of which has depended only on the enterprise of those engaged in it.—The English shipping industry has largely increased since the repeal of the Navigation Laws and the introduction of free trade, while the American shipping trade has been almost taxed out of existence under the United States tariff.—Although the French subsidies on navigation are avowedly granted, not for protective purposes, but to compensate shipowners for the "charges imposed on the mercantile navy for the recruitment and service of the military navy," and therefore in that respect do not come within the scope of this work, they are nevertheless so arranged as to protect the French shipping interest, as the subsidy on the navigation of a French-built ship is twice as great as that on a foreign-built ship.—The effect of this arrangement.—Subsidies on shipping sometimes defended abroad on the ground that England has

given similar assistance to her shipping trade in the form of
postal subsidies.—The essential difference between subsidies on
shipbuilding and postal subsidies explained .   .   *Pages* 18—38

PART II.—*Restraints on Imports.*

The difference between an import duty imposed for purposes of
revenue, and one imposed to protect home industry against
foreign competition.—The import duties levied in England have
no protective influence.—The home trader enjoys a kind of
natural protection in his own market, as the cost of carriage is
less in the case of home than in that of foreign produce.—It is
important to distinguish between the effect exerted by a protective duty in the country in which it is imposed, and its
effect on the countries from which produce subject to the duties
is imported. — The consequences of the protection formerly
given to agriculture in England.—It was generally supposed that
the continuance of high prices secured industrial prosperity, and
it was consequently thought that the profits of all concerned in the
cultivation of the land increased with the growing dearness of
agricultural produce.—Protective duties were not simply imposed
on corn ; live stock, fresh meat, and various other articles were
excluded altogether from our markets.—Attempts were made
to encourage the growth of British wool and flax by placing
difficulties in the way of the manufacture of cotton in England.
—The enactment of the Corn Laws after the fall in prices consequent on the peace of 1815.—The evils associated with the
sliding-scale.—The influence exerted by protection in England
upon the classes concerned in agriculture.—The farmers derived
no benefit from the high prices of agricultural produce, as each
rise in prices immediately led to an increase in rents.—Between
1815 and 1845, when the Corn Laws were in operation, agriculture was in a state of exceptional depression, and was frequently
the subject of inquiry by Parliamentary Committees.—Meeting
at Colchester, July, 1843.—Speech of Mr. Cobden, by which
many tenant farmers were convinced they had been injured by the
Corn Laws.—Deterioration in the condition of the agricultural
labourers.—Although protection led to an increase in the price
of agricultural produce, the competition of capital seeking investment prevented the farmers gaining more than the normal
rate of profit.—The depression in agriculture, though to a considerable degree brought about by the undue extent to which
rents were raised after the passing of the Corn Laws, and also
by the operation of the old Poor Law, was mainly owing to the

CHAPTER III.

FREE TRADE, FAIR TRADE, AND RECIPROCITY.

The economic advantages produced by free trade are the same, whether the exchange of commodities is between different countries, or between different parts of the same country.— Examination of the argument that, although interference with the freedom of trade between different parts of the same country would be indefensible, protection may be expedient, when it is confined to restricting the importation from other countries of articles which come into successful competition with those of home production.—Protective duties produce the same effects, whether the industry of any particular locality is protected

against home or foreign competition ; in support of this conclusion the question considered, Whether it is less advantageous for
the people of France to trade freely with Alsace and Lorraine
at the present time, than it was before these provinces were an-
nexed to Germany?—Supposing protective duties to be imposed
on articles imported from Alsace, it may be argued that the
French people would be compensated for the loss resulting from
their having to pay higher prices for these articles, because a
new industry would be brought into existence in France.   This
however implies that some branch of trade is being carried on in
a locality where the labour and capital employed in it do not
yield the maximum results.—Although the French may urge
that, as Alsace is now a part of Germany instead of a part of
France, it would be to their advantage to injure Alsace, the
economic loss to France of discouraging some industry most
suited to Alsace is the same whether Alsace is, or is not, part of
France.—Protection only defensible on the supposition that it is
advantageous for a country to make pecuniary sacrifices in order
to injure the prosperity of its neighbours.—Consideration of the
alleged impolicy on the part of England in permitting foreign
countries, which impose protective duties on her products, to
send their goods freely to her markets.—English trade is more
severely injured by the American than by any other tariff, the
protective duties imposed in the United States being largely in
excess of those levied in any other country.—Examination of the
proposal that England should retaliate on America by levying
import .duties on American goods. The exports of manufactured articles from the United States to England are so small,
that England could only produce any practical effect on American
trade by imposing duties on the various articles of food and
raw material imported from America. Any loss we could inflict
on America by such a policy would be trifling in comparison
with the loss we should inflict on ourselves.—The argument that
retaliation may be carried out when an article imported from some
country that maintains protection comes into competition with
an article of the same kind produced at home.—The alleged injury
to English trade arising from the importation of iron from
Belgium.—Further examples to show that it is impracticable
for England to carry out a policy of "reciprocity."—The effect
that would be produced by the adoption of a policy of
"reciprocity," if it were possible to carry it out.—A policy
of "reciprocity" would have aggravated the recent depression
in English trade   .   .   .   . *Pages* 62—88

CHAPTER IV.

THE ARGUMENTS OF PROTECTIONISTS.

CHAPTER V.

COMMERCIAL DEPRESSION.

The confidence felt in England in the advantages of a free-trade policy having increased with the growth of English prosperity, and been mainly supported by appeals to that prosperity, the recent depression in trade produced a disposition among some persons to lapse into the fallacies of protection.—In a similar manner, depressed trade in America led many of the advocates of protection in that country to doubt its efficacy to secure commercial prosperity.—The strength of this change of opinion shown by the proposal in 1878 of a new tariff.—A comparison of the commercial position of the United States and of England, respectively, shows that this country has no reason to waver in its adherence to a free-trade policy.—The greater severity of the depression in trade in America, in spite of the greater natural advantages of that country, is shown by the fact that during the depression the emigration from this country to America greatly declined, and was little greater than the emigration from America to this country.—The temporary falling-off in the export trade of England is due to a decline in the foreign demand, and not to our being driven out of neutral markets by the competition of protectionist countries.—The fears that have been lately expressed in this country at the large excess of imports over exports, considered.—This alarm has been increased by the fact that in hardly any other country is there any great excess of imports over exports, while in the United States the exports considerably exceed the imports.—The excess of imports in England to a great extent due to the fact, that in the statistical tables of English trade, the value at which any article imported is estimated includes the cost of carriage and the profit of the importing merchant ; whereas, in estimating the value of the exports, both the cost of carriage and the profit of the exporting merchants are excluded.—This fact to a considerable extent accounts for the excess of exports over imports in America as compared with the excess of imports over exports in England. —This excess of imports in England is also owing to the circumstance that no other country has so large an amount of capital embarked in foreign investments.—The dread expressed in England on the subject is probably a survival from the Mercantile System.—The excess of imports over exports in any country may be regarded as a measure of the extent to which it is a creditor of other countries.—That the excess of imports over exports in England is due to the circumstances before explained, is shown by the statistics of the English exports and imports of bullion and specie in recent years.—Although it is impossible to doubt that not long since there was very severe depression in many branches of English industry, there is reason to believe that the effects of the depression in trade in this country have been exaggerated, and that they were considerably greater in protectionist countries, such as America.—The increase in the English importation of articles of general consumption, such as tea.—A consideration of the effects produced by industrial activity, in some special trades, on the general body of the people.—The exceptionally high profits prevalent during the activity in the iron and coal trades, a few years since, were obtained at the expense of the general community.—The price of coal having, in consequence of the industrial depression, fallen to its former level, the country has been relieved of a serious burden.—This relief to the general body of the people may be regarded as some compensation for the losses brought on certain special classes by the depression in trade. —From the decline in pauperism, the maintenance of the Savings Banks deposits, and the increase . in the traffic returns of the railways, it may be concluded that the inactivity in some special branches of trade produced less effect on the general condition of the country than is usually supposed.— A great portion of the additional wealth created when certain trades are unusually active being simply a transfer from the general community to a special class, the cessation of this activity

implies a corresponding benefit to the general community.—
All persons in receipt of fixed incomes being severely injured
by the inflation of prices which takes place in a period
of great industrial activity, they are consequently benefited
by the fall in prices which occurs when trade declines.—The
recent depression in many branches of English trade was not,
as is often supposed, the result of the free-trade policy of
England, but was the natural outcome of the exceptional prosperity these trades enjoyed a few years since.—This conclusion
illustrated by a reference to the English coal trade.—Unless
an industry becomes depressed in consequence of a permanent
falling off in the demand, the depression cannot permanently
continue.—Reasons for this conclusion.—A portion of the remuneration secured by capital and labour in a time of exceptional
activity should be regarded as a reserve to meet the reduction
which is certain to ensue.—Depression may be produced by
many other causes quite as independent of free trade as the
one which has been considered; for example, a change in
fashion, or the development of a new machine.—The decline of the Spitalfields silk industry when the silk trade
was still protected is an illustration of this fact.—The present depression in English agriculture is far more due to unpropitious seasons than to foreign competition, as the prices
of agricultural products, with the exception of wheat and wool,
were higher between 1870 and 1880 than they were between
1830 and 1840, when the Corn Laws were in operation. Although bad seasons cause severe loss to the capital invested in
agriculture, the suffering to the rest of the community is restricted within the narrowest possible limits when the deficiencies
in our own crops can be supplied by free importation from other
countries.—The cultivator as distinguished from the owner has
no interest in the maintenance of high prices.—If foreign importations should increase there may be a permanent fall in
agricultural prices, necessitating a permanent reduction in rents,
and consequently a fall in the value of land in England.—The
foreign importations will most probably bring about a change
in the system of agriculture.—The reduction in the cost of
living, consequent on the fall in prices, has greatly contributed
to enable the country to tide over the period of industrial
depression.—The protectionist policy of America, by increasing the price of numerous commodities (import duties
being imposed by the American tariff on 1,500 different
articles), prevents this compensating influence coming into

operation.—The great increase of pauperism in the United States, and the disastrous losses sustained by the American railways, afford conclusive evidence that the depression in trade produced much more serious results in that country than in England.—A comparison, favourable to this country, may also be drawn between the commercial condition of free-trade England during a period of depression, and that of various other countries, such as Germany, Russia, and France, where restrictive tariffs are maintained.—The effects of depression on the Continent are aggravated by the strain resulting from the enormous armies maintained by the European powers.—Hence, the conclusion that a free-trade policy diminishes the effect of industrial depression is most strikingly corroborated by the comparison which has been made between the condition of England and that of America   . *Pages* 135—174

CHAPTER VI.

COMMERCIAL TREATIES.

The desirability of entering into a commercial treaty does not depend simply on economic considerations, as social and political advantages may be secured which will compensate for any disadvantage involved in the departure from sound economic principles.—It has been maintained by many high authorities, notably by Lord Overstone and Lord Grey, that the negotiation of a commercial treaty by a free trade country like England involves some sacrifice of principle, and that if the lowering or raising of the import duties, the character of which is determined solely by considerations of revenue, is made to depend on the tariff changes which may be introduced by other countries, a certain sanction is given to a policy of reciprocity.—The opponents of commercial treaties also lay stress on the limitations which they may impose on freedom of action with regard to future fiscal changes.—These disadvantages may be regarded as some compensation if the present negotiations for the renewal of the commercial treaty with France should fail.—A prominent economic advantage of commercial treaties is the opportunity the negotiations afford of representing to foreign protectionists the case in favour of free trade.—The increase in the trade between England and France under the commercial treaty of 1860.—The opposition in France to the renewal of the treaty based on the so-called "unfavourable balance of trade."—Consideration of the proposal that in the event of the present negotiations with France failing, England should "retaliate," and should impose a duty on some article of luxury imported from France, such as silk, or, by imposing export duties, should raise the price to the French consumer of such English products as coal or machinery.—General conclusion that England could not carry out a policy of retaliation without seriously injuring her own trade.—The protective system of foreign countries, though disadvantageous to our own trade, is accompanied by some compensating advantages, as protectionist countries cannot compete successfully with England in neutral markets. This conclusion established by reference to the export trade of England, the United States and France, respectively, to India and China.—The grounds of the demand made by English manufacturers for the repeal of the Indian import duties on cotton goods examined.—Although the tax must be condemned on economic grounds, the subject cannot be regarded as one involving economic considerations only.—In deciding the question as to the repeal of these duties the position of Indian finance must be taken into account.—Although many English Colonies maintain a system of protection far more onerous in its character than that involved in the retention of the Indian cotton duties, it has not been proposed that the Colonies should abolish their duties in the interests of English manufacturers.—In many of the appeals that are made for the repeal of the Indian cotton duties the interest of the manufacturers, as producers, is considered ; the interest of the people, as consumers, is ignored . *Pages* 175—192

FREE TRADE AND PROTECTION.

FREE TRADE AND PROTECTION.

CHAPTER I.

INTRODUCTORY REMARKS.

THE chief object I have in view in these pages is to endeavour to explain the causes which have not only retarded the general adoption of free trade, but have given a fresh vitality to the doctrines of protection. In no country where protection has been established does there seem to be any immediate prospect of the system being relinquished; on the contrary, in almost every instance tariffs have lately been made more protective. It is worthy of special remark that since 1877, with the single exception of Holland, where import duties have been steadily reduced, the tariffs of almost every European country, including Germany, Austria, Russia, Italy, Spain, Portugal and Greece, have all become more protective. The general tariff which has lately been proposed in France is more protective than the one it will replace, and a strong protectionist policy prevails in many of our colonies, especially in Victoria and Canada. Although during this period the tendency in the United States has been rather to reduce than to increase the duties, heavier protective duties are still imposed in the United States than in any other country.

B

Although it may be hoped that there is no danger of England departing from a policy of free trade, yet even here, where a few years since scarcely a single person could be found to say a word against free trade, a movement in opposition to what is called "one-sided free trade" is now finding many supporters.   It would be useless to deny that the strong position which is thus occupied by protection has surprised no less than disappointed those who have been the leading advocates of free trade in England.   Nothing could exceed the confidence with which it was predicted that when England had once enjoyed the advantages of unrestricted commerce, other countries would be led to follow her example by the irresistible force of self-interest. During the memorable debates which took place in 1846, when the financial reforms of Sir Robert Peel were before Parliament, it was again and again unhesitatingly asserted that all commercial countries would soon be eagerly striving to share with England the advantage of buying in the cheapest, and selling in the dearest market.   Even as recently as 1860, when the French commercial treaty was on the eve of ratification, its author declared that "nothing would be able to withstand the moral contagion of the example of England and France acting together on the principles of free trade;" and he predicted that the stimulus thus given to free trade "would extend far beyond the limits of the two countries."   Instead of these anticipations being realised, it would seem that the renewal of the commercial treaty with France, and the establishment of similar treaties with other countries, will now have to contend with even more opposition from protectionists than had to be encountered when that treaty was first proposed.

I think it desirable thus to direct special attention to the firm hold which protectionist doctrines have obtained, because nothing is more likely to retard the cause of free trade than to underrate the strength of the forces which are arrayed against it, and to ignore the circumstances on

which its opponents rely for support. It is unfortunate
that in discussing the subject English free-traders frequently
adopt a tone which is not calculated to convince those who
differ from them. When protectionists are spoken of as if
they were either solely prompted by a desire to sacrifice the
welfare of the community in order to promote their own
selfish ends, or when they are derided as the victims of
economic fallacies so transparent that they ought not to
mislead a child, it should be remembered that it is not many
years since the great majority of the English people were
ardent protectionists, and the fallacies for which so much
contempt is now often expressed were unhesitatingly accepted
by many of the most eminent of our countrymen. Little
more than forty years ago Lord Melbourne, who was then
Prime Minister, declared in the House of Commons, with
the cordial approval of the great majority of those whom
he addressed, that " during his long life it had been his lot
to hear many mad things proposed, but the maddest of all
the mad things to which he had ever had to listen was a
proposal to abolish the corn laws." Sir James Graham was
a statesman who had the reputation of possessing great
practical sagacity and much shrewd common sense.   A
deputation from Manchester waited upon him in 1840 to
urge the repeal of the corn laws, and in reply to their
arguments he said that " If the corn laws were repealed
great disasters would fall upon the country, that the
land would go out of cultivation, that Church and State
could not be upheld, that all our institutions would be
reduced to their primitive elements, and that the people
we were exciting would pull down our houses about our
ears." [1]   It cannot, I think, be denied that those who
endorsed this sweeping declaration in favour of protection
were not less misled by economic fallacies than are the
protectionists of the present day.   All the most effective

[1] *Cobden and the League*, by the late Mr. Henry Ashworth, of
Bolton, p. 42.

arguments that can now be urged in favour of free trade had many years previously been stated with the most admirable clearness and force by Adam Smith, Ricardo and other economists. In the pages of these writers are to be found many passages which furnish the best reply that can be made to the modern opponents of free trade. It may however be no doubt fairly urged that although little has of late been added to the theoretical arguments which can be advanced against protection, yet emancipation from the doctrines of this system was far more difficult before free trade had been tried, and that the striking success of the experiment in England ought to render a ready accept-ance of the true principles which should regulate the com-merce between nations indefinitely more easy. It should, however, be remembered that the adoption of free trade in England was powerfully promoted by circumstances of so purely exceptional a character that they do not now exist in any country where a protectionist tariff either has been, or is proposed to be, introduced. Between England and the countries which now maintain protection there is this fundamental distinction. In England it was agricul-tural produce that was most carefully protected, whereas in Continental countries, in America, and in the Colonies at the present time, it is home manufacturing industry that is most zealously shielded against foreign competition. In England, therefore, protection made such a first necessary of life as bread, dear ; whereas protection in those countries where it now exists increases the price of such commodities as wearing apparel and various articles of household furni-ture. It at once, therefore, becomes evident that a force of popular indignation could be brought against the mainten-ance of protection in England which cannot be brought against it in America and the Colonies. In a period of scarcity and of popular distress such as existed in England in 1843-45 the appeal in favour of free trade became irresistible. Every one who was suffering the pangs of hunger, every one who was pinched by want, could be told, "Bread is made dear, and starvation is brought upon you because the cheap wheat which foreign countries eagerly wish to send you is refused admittance to your ports." No such plea in favour of free trade can be brought home to the people of the United States. It may be impressed upon them that they pay a needlessly high [price for various manufactured commodities; that cloth, linen, shoes, hardware and innumerable other articles are made dearer by protection; but having to pay a higher price for a coat, a shirt or a hat, can never arouse the same popular indignation as when, in time of scarcity, the people find themselves deprived of the food they urgently need.

It no doubt may be said that protective duties were not in England solely imposed on agricultural produce, for when Sir Robert Peel propounded his free-trade policy, more than a thousand articles were subjected to import duties, many of which were protective in their character. It is, however, clearly shown by the tone of the discussions at the time, that the free-trade movement in England derived its chief impulse from the direct influence exerted by protection in raising the price of food. In the protracted debates in the House of Commons, speech after speech was made both by the opponents and the supporters of free trade, in which no reference was made to any other subject but the repeal of the corn laws. Sir Robert Peel again and again vainly tried to place the discussion on a wider basis by reminding Parliament that he proposed not simply to carry out the principle of free trade in reference to the importation of corn, but that he also intended to repeal every other protective duty. In the political history of our country it has been repeatedly shown that what is refused to reason is not unfrequently conceded to fear. Many, like Sir Robert Peel himself, who for so long had turned a deaf ear to the most cogent arguments that were adduced in favour of free trade, might have remained unconvinced and unconverted, had not a threatened famine in Ireland made them quail before the responsibility of maintaining a system which, by lessening the supplies of food, would have added to the number of those who were suffering the horrors of starvation. A short time before the abolition of protection there seemed to be every reason to suppose that the struggle might be long continued. The protectionist party had a large majority in both Houses of Parliament, and even of those who were not classed as protectionists a considerable number supported some modified form of protection, such for instance as an 8s. fixed duty on corn. The ultimate success of the free-trade movement in England was no doubt greatly due to the remarkable zeal and ability displayed by Mr. Cobden, Mr. Bright, Mr. W. J. Fox and other prominent leaders of the free-trade movement; but without in the slightest degree underrating the services thus rendered, it must be remembered that a speaker or a writer who desires at the present time to convince the American or Australian people of the injurious effects of protection has to employ very different illustrations, has to use very different arguments, and has to make very different appeals from those which in the days of the Anti-Corn-Law League exercised such irresistible influence in England. The belief became at that time firmly implanted in the public mind that the very hour protection was abolished food would become cheaper, and that so far as the great mass of the people were concerned, the blessing of this increased plenty would be accompanied by no qualifications, by no counter-balancing disadvantages. I shall have occasion to show that in consequence of a difference in economic circumstances the arguments now to be advanced in favour of free trade must be very different on the Continent, in America and in the Colonies to what they were in England before protection had been abandoned.

However great may be the ultimate advantages which free trade would confer, it is too often forgotten that when a great number of different manufactures have been artificially fostered, and have been forced into a kind of unnatural existence through protection, much suffering and loss may be caused to those who are engaged, either as employers or employed, in these particular industries, if the support they have derived from protection is withdrawn. There are no doubt many who will not agree in the opinion just expressed; for it is often maintained that the abolition of protection is sure to bring an increase of prosperity to those trades which are protected. It will not, I think, be difficult hereafter to show that this opinion is erroneous. It is, in fact, one of those instances which frequently occur of an economic principle being stated with too much generalisation, and without the necessary qualifications. It is thus often asserted that the introduction of a new machine must prove beneficial to the labourer. In one sense this no doubt is true, for probably on no portion of the community does the extended use of machinery ultimately confer so much advantage as on the labourer. Numerous examples, however, might be given from which it would be at once seen that the invention of a new machine has inflicted a real and severe loss upon some special class of labourers. The primary result of a mechanical invention is that it enables some industrial process to be mechanically performed which has previously required the exercise of manual skill. This skill can often only be acquired after a long and expensive training, and those who possess it are virtually the owners of property, the pecuniary value of which can be estimated by the extra wages which they receive when compared with the wages which are paid to the ordinary unskilled workman. It has, for instance, been stated that many of those who were most skilled among the Sheffield file-grinders have been able to earn as much as 6*l.* a week. Suppose a machine is invented which cuts files as well as they were previously cut by hand. The workman will then find that the necessity for his special skill has been altogether superseded. It

therefore ceases to possess any pecuniary value. He will
have to seek some employment in which he will have no
exceptional advantage which will enable him to claim
unusually high wages, and it will not improbably happen
that he may be unable to earn more than half the wages
which he had previously obtained. Great therefore as may
be the advantage conferred on a community by the extended
use of machinery in adding to the productiveness of labour
and capital, it is well not to lose sight of the fact that the
labourers whose special skill is superseded by a mechanical
invention may have to bear a loss as real as if the owner of
an estate should suddenly find his land deprived of half
its natural fertility.

When investigating the causes which induce such powerful
support to be given to the continuance of protection in
America and other countries, I think it can be shown that
the opposition to the adoption of a free-trade policy is to
a considerable extent prompted by motives very analogous
to those which have often induced the workmen employed
in some special trade to resist the introduction of a new
machine. The advocate of free trade, it will be pointed
out, has often a peculiar difficulty to encounter, because
the more striking and complete the advantages which would
result from the abolition of protection in any particular
industry, the greater the inducement offered to all those
engaged in this industry to resist the change. Thus in
order to bring into the strongest relief the loss which protection afflicts on a nation, some instances may be selected
where the circumstances of a country are so unfavourable
for the carrying on of a particular industry that it would
not exist at all if it were not secured against foreign competition by protective duties. In consequence of the productive salt mines possessed by England it is probable that
all the salt which the French consume would be obtained
from this country, and not a pound of salt would be manufactured in France, if extremely high protective duties

were not imposed on the importation of salt into that country. If, therefore, these duties were abolished, the manufacture of salt in France would cease to exist as an industry, and those who are engaged in it, either as masters or workmen, would have to bear the loss and inconvenience which always accompany the transfer of capital and labour· from one employment to another. In countries which maintain a system of protection there are always many industries, the existence of which, like the manufacture of salt in France, depends upon the continuance of protection. Any proposal therefore to abolish protection not unnaturally excites the combined opposition of all those who are concerned in these industries. Their opposition, prompted by self-interest, can hardly be expected to be removed, but, on the contrary, is not unfrequently increased, by the very strength of the facts which are adduced in favour of free trade. Thus it has been stated by the well-known American economist, Mr. D. A. Wells, that the people of the United States have to pay, in consequence of the protective duties on imported steel, such a needlessly high price for the steel rails they use, that it would be a remunerative expenditure if these protective duties were abolished, and if, out of state funds, the existing Bessemer steel works were purchased, and then closed, those employed in them receiving a pension in the way of compensation. Those, however, who have an interest in these works know perfectly well that they would have no chance of obtaining such compensation, and consequently the more they hear about the great reduction in price which would result from the free importation of steel, the more they become impressed with the loss which would be inflicted upon them, and consequently their opposition is intensified rather than appeased. I think we are able thus at least in part to understand why free trade has made such slow progress in those countries where protection has been long established, and where consequently it is supposed that many branches of industry depend upon the continuance of the system not only for their prosperity, but in many cases for their very existence.

Another phase, however, of the present protectionist movement seems at first sight more difficult to explain. Allusion has already been made to the strong support which is given to protection, and to the adoption of its principles, in many of our colonies. It may with reason be said, "It is possible to understand why in a country in which protection has long existed there should be many people prompted by a feeling of self-interest to advocate its maintenance; but how does it happen that in Victoria, for instance, which has been mainly peopled by those who have emigrated from free-trade England, there should be so widespread a feeling in favour of protection?" Considerable encouragement has no doubt been given to colonial protectionists by the opinions which have been expressed by some eminent economists, that the imposition of a protective duty with the view of promoting a new industry in a recently settled country may be justified as a temporary expedient. I shall not only have occasion to examine the theoretical arguments that are advanced in support of this opinion, but I think very conclusive facts may be adduced which show that the industries which are thus protected are ultimately injured rather than benefited. Enterprise and self-reliance are sure to be disastrously weakened if whenever some vicissitude in a trade occurs those who are engaged in it are taught to seek a remedy in higher protective duties. Moreover, all experience shows that although these protective duties are plausibly defended as a temporary expedient, yet, when they have been once imposed, they have never afterwards been voluntarily surrendered. From the moment any trade is protected a powerful vested interest is created, which is at once ready to combine with all the other protected interests in the country to resist any attempt to restore commercial freedom.

Amongst other circumstances which· probably cause protection to find favour in a young colony there is one to which, as I believe it has attracted little notice, it will be desirable here briefly to refer. A large portion of the population of such a colony as Victoria is composed of those who have emigrated from England. Amongst these· emigrants there are sure to be many who will discover that they cannot find the same kind of employment as that to which they have been accustomed. An intending emigrant would of course act more wisely if, before leaving, he ascertained whether he was likely to obtain any suitable work in the country in which he proposed to settle. These precautions, however, are often entirely neglected. When intelligence was first brought to this country that rich deposits of gold had been discovered in Australia, thousands who had never done a day's out-door work eagerly rushed to the gold-fields. As time went on it was discovered that the gold-digger's lot was by no means so desirable a one as it was supposed to be; his labour was severe; he had to endure many hardships; he had often to suffer much exposure; and although, here and there, there was one who by some stroke of good fortune quickly became rich, yet the gold-digger did not on the average obtain an exceptionally high remuneration for his labour. Under these circumstances it is evident that Australia presented a favourable field for the growth of protection. Those who before they had emigrated from England had been employed as operatives or artizans in some manufactory or workshop would be sure soon to find that they were unsuited for such work as gold-digging. They would naturally therefore welcome any proposal to establish through the aid of protective duties some kind of industry similar to that in which they had been employed before they emigrated. A prospect would thus be offered to them of obtaining work to which they had been accustomed, and they would again be able to turn to advantage any special skill which in previous years they had acquired.

If, as just indicated, I attempt in the following pages fairly to consider the causes which have not only retarded the general adoption of free trade, but which have even created a certain reaction in favour of protection, I hope it will not be supposed that I wish in the slightest degree to defend the protective system or to palliate the mischief which it produces. I feel however very strongly the importance of giving full and careful consideration to the arguments that are advanced by protectionists. It has I believe not infrequently happened that the opposition to free trade has been strengthened rather than weakened by the tone in which the subject has been discussed. It is never well to underrate the forces of an antagonist; and when it is observed that almost every country except England favours protection, and that even in England opinions are held to which practical effect could not be given without reintroducing some form of protection, it must be acknowledged that the time has certainly come when it is desirable carefully to review the 'position assumed by the opponents of free trade. It is the more important that this should be done because the line of argument which is often adopted by the advocates of free trade is not the one which is best calculated to bring conviction to those who differ from them. It will for instance be observed that scarcely a week elapses without some speech being made or some essay written in which the increase which has taken place in the wealth of England since 1846 is attributed entirely to the influence of free trade. When it is shown that during this period the commerce of England has had such a prodigious . development that her aggregate exports and imports have more than quadrupled, it should be remembered that almost contemporaneously with the adoption of free trade other causes came into operation which have produced a powerful effect in promoting this growth of prosperity. Thus it may be mentioned that up to that time the plan had been tenaciously adhered to, of raising revenue from almost every article of foreign produce that was imported. In 1845 import duties were levied upon no less than 1142 separate articles. Of the duties which were thus imposed only those could be considered protective which placed the foreign producer at a disadvantage compared with the home producer. A large number of the articles imported, such as tea, coffee, chicory, sugar, and wine, are not produced in England, and consequently the duties which were imposed upon them could not be protective in their character. When it is remembered that, by a series of fiscal reforms with which the names of Sir Robert Peel and Mr. Gladstone will always be associated, the duties on these 1142 articles have, with barely a dozen exceptions, been repealed—our customs' revenue being now almost entirely raised from five articles, tea, coffee, tobacco, spirits, and wine—it at once becomes evident that the incalculable advantages resulting from the financial reforms which were carried out in England cannot be solely attributed to the abolition of protection. It is also to be borne in mind that about the time when protection was abolished the railway system was beginning to be developed, steam was being more largely used as a motive power in industry, and the discovery of gold in Australia and California, by stimulating emigration and in various other ways, assisted the production of wealth. In order to show the fallacy involved in attributing the whole of the increase in wealth since 1846 to the abolition of protection, it is sufficient to remark that without railways so large an increase would have been impossible, and that when many causes combine to promote national prosperity, one ought not to be singled out and spoken of as if it alone had been in operation. Such a method of reasoning not only admits of an easy reply, but is calculated to do serious injury to the cause of free trade. It is only necessary to refer to the United States, to France and other protective countries which enjoy great prosperity, to show that the increased production of wealth depends on other causes besides free trade. If the English free-trader rests his case upon the increase of wealth in his own country, he is immediately met with the rejoinder that with tariffs that have gradually become more protective there has also been a great increase of wealth in the United States and other countries. Little practical good can result from thus arraying the prosperity of one country against that of another. All that can fairly be deduced from such comparisons is that whereas the production of wealth is stimulated by free trade and is retarded by protection, the economic conditions of a protective country may be in other respects so favourable that although protection may impede, it cannot arrest its progress.

There is the more reason for avoiding the line of argument to which allusion has just been made because the habit which had become so general of attributing all our prosperity to free trade has undoubtedly produced at the present time in England a certain reaction in favour of protection. There are many who, still professing to be free traders, object to what is termed one-sided free trade ; they say that free trade is excellent if it is universal, but England places herself in an unfair position if whilst other countries refuse admission to her products, she freely admits theirs to her ports. A demand has consequently arisen for "fair trade" as a substitute for free trade. I shall have occasion in a subsequent chapter to consider the various proposals based upon the principles of reciprocity or retaliation, for giving effect to this demand. The subject has, however, been thus briefly referred to here with the object of showing that if a people are accustomed to believe that free trade is the sole cause of national prosperity they not unnaturally, when there is any reverse, single out free trade as the cause of industrial depression. A similar change of opinion in an opposite direction occurred in the United States a few years since. The depression in that country about the years

1876-77 was even more severe than it was in England, and many who before had been warm adherents of protection were then induced to doubt its efficacy. Although free trade cannot prevent fluctuations in the industrial progress of a country, yet I think it can be shown that if our commerce had been in any way less unrestricted than it is, the depression from which England has recently been suffering would have been indefinitely greater, and would have been accompanied by incalculably more severe hardship to the mass of the people. Facts will be subsequently adduced which will show even with regard to agriculture, severe as are the losses which have been borne during the last few years by farmers and landowners, yet that during the period when the corn laws were in operation and when the importation of wheat was prohibited until its price reached 70s. a quarter, there were many periods of depression at least as severe as that through which we are now passing. The losses of the farmers were quite as great, and whereas the labourers throughout the present period of depression have been comparatively well off, they were often reduced during the time of the corn laws to a state of wretchedness which it is now difficult to imagine.

Having now in these introductory remarks indicated the general character of the inquiry it is intended to make in the following pages, I shall proceed in the next chapter to consider the theory of protection. It is important to restate the principles on which free trade rests, because, as previously remarked, not only is there at the present time little progress being made towards the acceptance of these principles in protectionist countries, but even in England they are in many quarters so imperfectly understood that demands are now frequently made which, if they were conceded, would soon involve the trade of the country in a labyrinth of protectionist trammels. As a further illustration of the fact that the real nature of the advantages conferred by free trade is often very inadequately appreciated even in

England, reference may again be made to the fact that the protectionists in Australia, Canada and other Colonies have been largely recruited by those who have lately emigrated from England. It not unfrequently happens that a Lancashire or Yorkshire operative, who had in England always been an ardent free-trader, almost immediately becomes a not less ardent protectionist when he settles in the Colonies, and is there surrounded by a different set of economic circumstances.

A discussion of the theory of protection will naturally divide itself into a consideration of the two different ways in which effect has been given to a policy of protection, namely by the granting of bounties on exports, and by the imposition of protective import duties. Although bounties on exports are now much less frequently resorted to by protectionist countries than protective import duties, yet the subject of bounties is one possessing much practical interest at the present time, in consequence of the bounties given on the export of sugar by many Continental countries. Bounties on shipping were also recently (1881) introduced by France, with the object of encouraging her mercantile marine. In connection with these bounties many interesting questions arise, for it will be shown that they are, in part at least, given as a subsidy to French shipbuilders to compensate them for the loss inflicted on their trade by a protectionist tariff. A consideration of the subject of protective import duties will afford an opportunity of discussing the various projects which are now so constantly brought forward in England of correcting what are supposed to be the disadvantages of one-sided free trade. I think it will be shown that serious as may be the injury which is inflicted on England by the protectionist tariffs of other countries, this injury, far from being diminished, would be indefinitely aggravated if, in a spirit of retaliation, reciprocal duties were imposed.

After having thus considered the general theories of free

trade and protection, I shall endeavour in a subsequent chapter to give a full and impartial statement of all the leading arguments which are advanced in America, the Continent, and the Colonies in favour of protection. These arguments will be classed under thirteen heads, each of which will be separately considered. In the two concluding . chapters, the subjects of commercial depression and commercial treaties will be dealt with; and I think with regard to commercial depression it will be easy to prove that this depression has not been caused by free trade, that many countries whose tariffs are highly protective have felt this depression far more severely than England, and that without free trade the losses to English commerce, and the consequences to her people generally, would have been incalculably more serious.

CHAPTER II.

PART I.—*Bounties on Exports, and Protective Subsidies.*

THE chief advantage which protectionists claim for the system they support is that it gives encouragement and assistance to native industry. Protection was defended in England, and is still defended in the countries where it is maintained, on the ground that various home industries would inevitably decline if, unaided by protective duties, they had to contend against foreign competition. Although this desire to protect the home trader against his foreign rival may no doubt be regarded as the chief cause why protectionist tariffs have been maintained, yet many duties, which have been most protective in their character, were in the first instance imposed not with any idea of encouraging native industry, but with the very different object of securing what is called a "favourable balance of trade." Until a period which is marked by the publication of Adam Smith's *Wealth of Nations*, 1775, it was almost universally assumed that the advantage or disadvantage which foreign commerce conferred upon a country was solely to be measured by the extent to which her stock of the precious metals was either increased or diminished. If the goods which a country imported exceeded in value those which were exported, then a balance was due from her to the countries with which she traded. Money consequently had to be transmitted abroad to adjust this balance; as it was supposed that the country was rendered so much poorer by the money which was thus sent away, it was thought to be an object of first importance that this flow of money should be checked, and, if possible, turned in an opposite direction. The encouragement of exports and the dis-- couragement of imports consequently became the guiding principle of the commercial policy of every country, because the more exports were increased and the more imports were diminished the greater would be the amount of money which would have to be received, and the less would be the amount which would have to be paid. One of the most general methods which were adopted for encouraging exports and discouraging imports, was to give a bounty on exports, and to impose heavy duties on imports. Those who sent produce abroad were considered to be such benefactors of their country that the money of the State could be well and fairly spent in rewarding them. Those, on the other hand, who imported produce would have to send money to foreign countries in payment for this produce. They consequently were regarded as con- cerned in transactions which would lead to national impoverishment; and it was therefore considered expedient to impede, by the imposition of duties or in any other way, the trade in which they were· engaged. But the policy having been once adopted of granting bounties on ex- ports, and of imposing restraints on imports, with the view of creating a favourable balance of trade, it gradually came to be seen that other consequences resulted from thus encouraging exports and impeding imports. It was considered that by adopting such a policy two distinct advantages would be secured. In the first place, native industry would be assisted; and secondly, the trade of foreign countries would be impeded. The home trader who received a bounty on the goods he exported might be enabled to undersell his foreign competitors in their own markets; whilst import duties, if made sufficiently high, would effectually keep out foreign competition from the home market. Commerce was so generally looked upon as a struggle between rival countries whose interests were assumed to be entirely antagonistic, that to impede the industrial development of foreign nations was supposed to be scarcely less important than to aid the prosperity of home trade. Even at the present time there are many who apparently think that it is to the direct interest of their own country that other nations should not prosper. It will, in fact, be shown when considering the arguments which are now advanced in support of protection, that the only logical basis on which the system can rest is the assumption that a conflict is being perpetually waged between countries which trade with each other, and that it is not less important in this industrial war than it would be in a struggle for military supremacy, to adopt every expedient in order to weaken the resources of the enemy.

The policy of protection is now so generally carried out by the imposition of import duties, that the subject of protection is not unfrequently discussed without any special reference being made to the protective influence which may be exerted by the granting of bounties on exports. In past times, however, these bounties played a very prominent part in the commercial policy of many countries, and even in recent times the granting of bounties, although it has been to a great extent discontinued, has not been entirely given up. It is well known that at the present day several Continental countries give a bounty on the export of sugar, and during the year 1881 a law was passed in France giving a bounty on French shipping. The subject, therefore, not only has an historical interest, but is one of so much practical importance that it will be desirable to direct attention to it. Adam Smith[1] says:—"Bounties upon exportation are, in Great Britain, frequently petitioned for,

[1] *Wealth of Nations,* Book iv. chap. 5.

and sometimes granted to the produce of particular branches of domestic industry. By means of them our merchants and manufacturers, it is pretended, will be enabled to sell their goods as cheap or cheaper than their rivals in the foreign market. A greater quantity, it is said, will thus be exported, and the balance of trade consequently turned more in favour of our own country." Although these bounties were petitioned for and granted on the ground that they would promote a favourable balance of trade, which at the time was supposed to constitute an advantage for the entire nation, yet there are clear indications that those who thus petitioned for these bounties were not solely influenced by an anxiety for the national weal. The spirit of protection can be distinctly traced in the policy which was then advocated ; for in the same chapter of the *Wealth of Nations* from which the above passage has been quoted, it is stated that manufacturers and other traders greatly favoured these bounties, because they not only enabled surplus stocks to be disposed of to foreigners, but through their agency prices in the home market were maintained at a high level. In numerous instances bounties were granted on the export of the very articles on which, when imported, high protective duties were imposed. A remarkable example of this is afforded by the high bounties which were for many years in England granted on the export of corn, at the time when its importation was restricted by the levying of onerous duties. It therefore happened that in years when there was a bountiful harvest, those who had corn to sell were bribed, at the public expense, to send it abroad ; and in years of scarcity the general public were prevented from buying the food which they urgently needed, and which other countries were willing to sell them, in order that those might be benefited who were interested in the maintenance of a high price for corn. It is impossible to devise any arrangement which would inflict a greater amount of injustice and suffering on a community. In the first place, the encouragement which was given to the sending of surplus corn abroad in good seasons left the country with a smaller accumulated store with which to meet times of scarcity. Secondly, bounties, by increasing the foreign demand for corn, increased its price to the home consumers, who were thus in this unfortunate position: they were taxed in order to raise the price of the food they consumed. It thus appears that the country was not only, through the operation of these bounties, placed in a more unfavourable position to meet the difficulties which had to be encountered in seasons of scarcity, but these difficulties were also greatly increased in consequence of food being made artificially dear through the restraints which were imposed on the importation of corn.

Although, therefore, it is evident that this system of granting bounties on exports, accompanied, as it was, with restraints upon imports, must have inflicted an incalculable amount of suffering on the nation, yet the policy was not, as we have seen, forced on a people unwilling to receive it; but, on the contrary, we are told that the Government was constantly petitioned, by those engaged in various trades, to favour them with a bounty. As this system of granting bounties is still maintained in France and other countries, it becomes of practical importance to inquire what is the general effect of these bounties, not only upon the countries in which they are granted, but on those countries to which the produce receiving the bounty is exported. Adam Smith has said that when a bounty was granted to any particular trade, those who were engaged in it considered that they were favoured by a special advantage. As it seems that the same opinion still prevails in countries where the system of bounties is continued, it will be desirable to ascertain what is the precise effect upon those who are concerned in the production of any particular commodity, the export of which is stimulated by bounties. This may be shown by tracing the effect of granting a bounty on the export of sugar from France; the effect of the bounties given on French shipping will be afterwards investigated. It is desirable to consider the subject of the French sugar bounties not only because of the interest excited by the question in England, but as beetroot, from which sugar is largely made in France, is grown' in France, the case will afford an opportunity of considering the influence exercised by a bounty, both upon a manufacturing and an agricultural industry.

Owing to the complicated and indirect way in which this bounty is received, there is a great divergence of opinion with regard to the amount which is annually expended upon it. The French Government allege that the bounty involves a charge on their revenue of about 360,000*l.*, whereas the English sugar refiners assert that the annual charge is not less than 750,000*l.*, or 800,000*l.* If a certain fixed sum were simply given on each ton of sugar exported, the amount of the charge would, of course, be at once known. The bounty is, however, received in such an indirect manner, that there is considerable difficulty in calculating its exact amount. A duty is in France charged on raw sugar in proportion to its estimated yield of refined sugar. In order, however, to encourage the French sugar-refining industry, the Government give a drawback on refined sugar, when it is exported, which is professed to be equivalent to the duty imposed on raw sugar. If the refiner received as a drawback upon the refined sugar which he exported an amount exactly equivalent to the duty which he paid on the raw sugar, it is obvious that he would receive no bounty on export, he would obtain from the Government no more than he had paid them. It is, however, alleged that the duties are calculated on such a basis, that the drawback which is given on the refined sugar exported exceeds by about ten per cent. the amount which is paid on the raw sugar. The duty is very high, being nearly equivalent to the value of the sugar, and it is calculated that the bounty, which is in this way given, amounts to about 3s. per cwt.[1] Such a bounty represents at least 10 per cent. of the value of the sugar exported. The French sugar manufacturers would of course be great gainers if they could appropriate to themselves the whole of this bounty; for in addition to the ordinary current rate of profit on the sugar which they sell for home consumption, they would obtain, as extra profit, ten per cent. on the entire amount which was sold for export. Such a business would evidently be so exceptionally remunerative, that each sugar manufacturer would eagerly strive to appropriate to himself as much as possible of the business so peculiarly lucrative. The result of this struggle must inevitably be to force down the price of the sugar exported; for the manufacturer would still be a considerable gainer if he obtained on each ton of sugar exported, 5s. more than if the sugar were sold at home. The effect of the bounty must, therefore, be to enable England and other foreign countries to purchase French sugar at a considerably lower price. This reduction in price will approximate to the amount of the bounty. The competition of the French sugar manufacturers amongst themselves will prevent them obtaining a larger profit on the sugar which is exported than upon that which is sold for home consumption; consequently the bounty, which is given by the French Government on the export of sugar, although intended to promote the prosperity of the French sugar trade, is really almost entirely spent in enabling the English people and others, who use French sugar, to enjoy the advantage of purchasing it at considerably below cost price. The French Government really act as if, prompted by a generous desire to make a gift to their foreign neighbours, they said to the sugar manufacturers in France: if you will sell to the English people and other

[1] See paper read by a leading English sugar refiner, Mr. George Martineau, at the Brighton meeting of the Social Science Association, 1875.

foreigners, such a useful article as sugar at considerably less than its cost price, we will compensate you by a Government grant for any loss which you may have to bear.

By thus artificially stimulating the export of sugar from France, the French sugar trade is no doubt extended, and the demand for French beet-root and other materials, out of which sugar is made, is increased. But when considering any attempts that may be made, either by bounties on exports, or by restraints on imports, to give an artificial encouragement to any particular trade, it cannot be too distinctly borne in mind that it is impossible permanently to secure an exceptionally high rate of profit to any branch of industry, unless free admission to it is barred, and those who are engaged in it enjoy the privileges of a close monopoly. In every commercial country there are always many who, possessing a large amount of floating capital, are constantly looking out for a lucrative investment; and water is not more certain to find its level than is this capital to flow into those channels where it can be used with the greatest advantage. If, therefore, by giving such a bounty as that on French sugar, it should be supposed that an amount equivalent to the bounty were added to the profits of a particular class of traders, there would be an eager rush of those who had capital to employ, to share in the exceptional gains yielded by this favoured branch of industry. There could be no certainty that this flow of capital would be kept within due control, and it might not improbably happen that those who were engaged in the trade on which the bounty is given would find that, instead of being a privileged class enjoying special advantages, the profits of their business had been reduced below the average rate, owing to the excessive amount of capital that had been attracted to it.

The price of the article, the export of which is stimulated by a bounty, will no doubt be generally raised; and this has probably led to the belief that bounties are particularly advantageous to the special class of traders who obtain them. Even Adam Smith, when referring to the bounties which in his time were given on corn, speaks as if farmers were specially benefited by the price of agricultural produce being maintained at a high level. It can, however, be shown that whenever the price of an article is artificially raised, either by encouraging exports or discouraging imports, the higher price does not represent an increased rate of profit, but is nothing more than a bare compensation given to the trader, because he has to carry on his industry at a greater cost. It has been already explained that capital is sure to be drawn to any trade which is supposed to yield an unusually high rate of profit; and thus the force of competition being ever present to exercise an equalising influence, will prevent a larger return from being realized from those trades which are protected, than from other industries carried on in the same country. When the corn laws were in operation in England, corn no doubt was made extremely dear; but it will be subsequently shown that during this period the English tenant-farmers were frequently in a most depressed condition. Committees were on several occasions appointed by Parliament to inquire into the causes of agricultural distress, and it was proved that as prices rose rents were advanced. Not only did this increase of rent absorb all the advantage which the farmers might have derived from the high prices which were created through protection, but a most serious injury was inflicted upon them by the very legislation which was presumably passed in their interest. The effect of the corn laws in raising prices was over-estimated; rents were calculated on a basis of high prices, which in the average of years were not maintained; and farmers consequently were unable to pay the rents which had been agreed upon. The only class, therefore, who can permanently profit from any particular produce being made artificially dear, are those who own the land on which the produce is grown, and not those who either rent it, or those who use the produce as the raw material of some manufacture. Thus the stimulus which is given to the export of French sugar by the present bounty may, by increasing the demand for beet-root from which this sugar is so largely made, increase its price, and thus additional value may be given to the land on which the beet-root is grown. But the gain which is in this way secured by a special class, is purchased at the expense of the entire French nation. The whole community is, in fact, doubly taxed. In the first place, the bounty, whether it costs 750,000l., or only 360,000l. a year, still represents a very serious charge which has to be borne by the entire body of French tax-payers. This charge, however, large though it is, can only be regarded as a portion of the burden which is thrown upon them; for if sugar is raised as little as a farthing a pound in France by this forced export, and this is a very moderate estimate, the additional price which the French will be compelled to pay for their sugar cannot be less than 1,000,000l. a year.

The chief results that are secured by the imposition of this onerous fine, are first, that more of the land, capital, and labour of France, are devoted to the growing of beet-root than would otherwise be the case, and the value of the land suitable for the growth of beet-root is somewhat enhanced; secondly, that French sugar is sold at a lower rate in England and other countries than it otherwise would be.

It would certainly seem that we should be the last to complain if the French are willing thus to tax themselves for our benefit. The English sugar refiners have, however, repeatedly endeavoured to induce our Government to interpose on their behalf, and to protect them against French competition by imposing on French sugar an import duty, which would neutralise the effect of the bounty. Considerable injury is no doubt inflicted on English sugar refiners by the French being bribed by their Government to sell sugar in the English market at a price which, without a State subvention, would not prove remunerative. If, however,

we once embarked on the policy of protecting a special trade
against the harm which may be done to it by some other
country adopting an unwise fiscal policy, we should soon
find ourselves involved in a labyrinth of commercial restrictions, and our tariff would become as protectionist as is the
tariff of the most protectionist country. We occasionally
hear of iron being imported into England from Belgium,
and of cotton goods being sent to us from America. Our
ports are freely open to receive any quantity of these products which America or Belgium may be willing to send
us; and yet our manufacturers find that they cannot export
a single ton of iron to Belgium, or a single bale of cotton
goods to the United States, without the payment of import
duties. If, therefore, English sugar refiners were protected
against the competition of cheap French sugar, English ironmasters and English cotton manufacturers would be able to
put forward an unanswerable claim to be secured against the
competition of their foreign rivals. It usually happens that
we, as a nation, obtain no compensating advantage for the
injury which is done us by the protectionist tariffs of other
countries. It can no doubt be shown that those who maintain these tariffs inflict a far greater injury upon themselves
than they do upon us; but it cannot be denied that the
English suffer, as a nation, by the commercial restrictions of
other countries. When, however, the encouragement to
home industry, which is supposed to be the main object
of protection, is secured, not by imposing restraints on
imports, but by granting bounties on exports, the loss
which such a policy entails does not extend beyond the
country which adopts it. England, as we have seen, gains,
as certainly as France loses, by the bounty on French
sugar; and as long as France is willing to tax herself for
our benefit, why should we refuse to accept the advantage
which is offered to us? We should be simply giving a new
sanction to protection if the import of cheap sugar from
France were impeded, with a view of causing such an

advance in the price of sugar as would make the trade of sugar-refining in England adequately remunerative.

It is desirable separately to consider the bounties which are now given in various countries on shipping, because it will be seen that the assistance thus granted to a special industry, produces consequences different from those which are produced by the bounties on exports to which attention has just been directed. As the policy of conferring bounties on shipping has recently received its most important development in France, the principles involved in the adoption of such a system can be best explained by describing in some detail the bounties which are now given on French shipping. By a law which was passed at the beginning of the year 1881 [1] a bounty, or, as it may be more correctly termed, a subsidy, is given both on the building and on the navigation of French ships—the subsidy on navigation to continue for ten years only. The subsidy given to the builders of iron or steel vessels is sixty francs per ton, to the builders of large wooden vessels twenty francs, and of small vessels ten francs. A subsidy is also given on the machinery used in steam vessels amounting to twelve francs per 100 kilog., equivalent to about 120 francs per ton. The subsidy on the navigation of French ships takes the form of a payment made to the owner of the ship of one franc and a half per register ton for each 1,000 miles 'run. As the subsidies which are thus respectively given on the building and navigation of ships are granted for very different reasons, it will be convenient to consider them separately.

In the fourth article of the law establishing the subsidies just described, and which is entitled the Mercantile Marine Law, it is stated that the subsidies given on the building of vessels are "to compensate ship-builders for the charges

[1] See Parliamentary Return, entitled, "Further Correspondence Relative to the French Mercantile Marine Bill." *Commercial*. No. 8. 1881.

fixed by the Custom House tariff;" and the object aimed
at is still more explicitly explained in the report of the
Committee of the Senate, appointed to consider the Bill
after it had been passed by the Chamber of Deputies.   It
is stated in this Report that the object of the measure is
to "facilitate the construction of ships by enabling ship-
builders to obtain duty free the metal, wood, &c., which
they require, this end being attained by giving them a
subsidy on the ships built equivalent to the duty."   In
defence of this policy it is with much persistency urged by
its advocates in France that it involves no infringement of
the principles of free trade, because foreign ships are still
to be freely admitted to French ports.   Although it may
not be intended to give any protection to French shipping,
yet I think it can be shown that these subsidies are a new
development of the protective system which may involve
very serious consequences to those countries which adopt
them.   As previously stated, the assistance given to home
industry through the agency of protection has hitherto been
confined to the granting of bounties on export, and to
discouraging by the imposition of import duties the competition of foreign with home products.   The assistance
however [which is given to a particular [industry by such
a subsidy as that now granted on the building of ships in
France assumes a very different character.   The object of
the subsidy in this case is to protect those engaged in a
particular industry from the injury which is inflicted on
them by their own Government.   The question therefore
is at once suggested: What are likely to be the consequences of carrying out this special form of protection?
And in answering this question it will obviously be necessary
to consider the effect upon those who enjoy the protection,
as well as the effect upon those who provide the funds from
which this protection, in the form of a pecuniary compensation, is given.   Dealing in the first instance with the
consequences involved in having to provide the amount

required for the subsidy, it might be remarked that the annual sum which is needed is estimated by the French Government to be about 1,400,000 francs,[1] but whether the amount be large or small it is evident that the money can be supplied from no other source except the general taxation of the country. It cannot be too constantly borne in mind that governments are just as powerless as ordinary individuals to create wealth except by an expenditure of labour and capital. This truth seems to be lost sight of in proposals that are frequently brought forward involving grants of public money. Not only have governments no power to create wealth at will, but with regard to the creation of wealth they are even in a less favourable position than ordinary individuals; for it invariably happens, in consequence of the cost involved in collecting taxation, that any tax which may be imposed takes more from the people than it yields to the state. By the granting of such a subsidy as that which we are now considering the whole community is taxed for the benefit of a special class. The same thing happens as if money were compulsorily taken from A, B, C, D, and E, in order to give it to F. But when this system of appropriating the money of the general community for the benefit of a special class or interest has been once commenced it will probably have to be extended without any assignable limits. If the builders of French ships are subsidised in order to compensate them for the extra expense to which they are subject in consequence of iron, wood, and other materials which they may use being made dearer through the imposition of protective import duties, almost every industry in the country may put forward a cogent claim to be subsidised. Dear iron and wood compel the French farmer to pay an unnecessarily high

---

[1] The amount of the bounty paid by the French Government up to the 1st of January, 1884, was 16,696,000 francs, or 668,000*l*. The amount demanded by the Minister of Commerce in his Budget Estimate for the year 1885 was 11,000,000 francs, or 440,000*l*.—M. G. F.

price for his ploughs, his threshing-machines and other implements; the cotton and the woollen manufacturers have to pay more for their machinery, and their buildings are erected at a greater cost; the wine-grower has to pay more for his casks; the railway companies more for their locomotives, their carriages and their rails. It may be urged that some of these industries already receive a subsidy in consequence of the advantage they derive from being protected in the home market against foreign competition. Thus the heavy import duties imposed upon woollen and cotton goods imported into France may perhaps be thought to confer upon the French woollen and cotton manufacturers an advantage which is equivalent to that obtained by the French ship-builders from the subsidy they now receive. It almost invariably happens that the prosperity of an industry does not simply depend upon the home demand. The French woollen and cotton manufacturers have not only to contend with the competition of their foreign rivals in their own markets; unless they are willing entirely to abandon their export trade, they have to contend with them in the neutral markets of the world, and in this competition outside the limits of 'France it is obvious that an import duty is powerless to provide the French manufacturers with the smallest compensation for the additional outlay they incur in consequence of the higher price they have to pay for machinery, iron, wood and all the other articles which they purchase and which are made unnecessarily dear.

Although these subsidies may not in the first instance lead to a very serious expenditure of public money, yet it may very possibly happen that the granting of them may produce consequences of the first importance. It has, I think, been shown that when the principle has once been conceded of devoting public money to compensate one particular industry for the injury inflicted upon it by the various duties which are imposed in order to carry out a protectionist policy, the claims of other industries which

suffer a similar injury to receive similar compensation will
be so cogent as to prove irresistible. The system of
subsidies may thus be gradually extended to almost every
trade, and if this is the case a most powerful agency must
inevitably be brought into operation to undermine the
protective system. It is difficult to imagine how the most
devoted adherent of protection can continue to believe in
its efficacy if he should find that it has brought about the
result that almost every industry has to be subsidised in
order, if possible, to provide some compensation for the
injury inflicted upon it by protection.

Returning, however, to the immediate subject of our
inquiry, it remains for us to consider what is likely to be
the effect of these subsidies on the ship-building trade. It
has already been shown, in referring to the consequences
produced by giving a bounty on exports, that the equalising
force of competition prevents the remuneration received by
the capitalist or labourer engaged in any particular industry
from being permanently higher than the profits and wages
obtained in other employments. The effect of the subsidy
will be not to give higher profits and wages to those
engaged in the ship-building trade, but to place the French
ship-builder in a position which will enable him to reduce the price at which he can sell his ships. The object
sought to be obtained by the subsidy is by lowering the
price of French ships to stimulate the French ship-building
trade. It therefore becomes desirable to ascertain what is
supposed to be the effect likely to be produced by the
stimulus thus given. In the report of the Committee of the
Senate, to which reference has already been made, it is
estimated that whilst the subsidy will do no more than
arrest the decline in the number of sailing vessels built,
it will exercise so much influence in stimulating the building
of French steam-ships that it will increase the tonnage of
the foreign-going steam-ships in the course of two years
from 120,000 to 200,000 tons. As this is said in the

Report to represent a "magnificent result which may be considered as a maximum," it becomes desirable to compare the effect produced upon the development of an industry by Government interference, with the development of the same industry when its progress, unaided by Government, depends upon the individual enterprise and skill of those who are engaged in it. The aggregate tonnage of the 'steam vessels possessed by Great Britain at the end of 1883 was 3,728,268 tons, and in a single year, between 1882-83, the addition made to the tonnage was no less than 393,053 tons—a larger tonnage than that which it is anticipated will represent the entire steam tonnage in the foreign-going mercantile marine of France even after an artificial stimulus has been given to it by the granting of subsidies.[1]

Although we have recently had to pass through a period of severe depression, the steam tonnage of Great Britain has considerably more than doubled in the last ten years, for in 1873 it amounted to only 1,713,783 tons. It was estimated in 1881 that England then possessed 49 per cent. of the ship-carrying power of the world, and with regard to steam vessels the proportion was still larger, being no less than 63 per cent.[2] We should be repeating an error to which allusion has already been made if this remarkable development of the English mercantile marine were wholly attributed to the fact that England is a free-trade country. Other causes have undoubtedly contributed to this result. Still, whatever may have been the extent to which other causes have operated, great significance is

---

[1] In 1883, the second year after the bounty had been in operation, the addition to the French Mercantile Marine was only 35,223 tons, or rather less than an eleventh of the addition to the English Mercantile Marine in the corresponding period.—M. G. F.

[2] See article on "The Carrying-Trade of the World," by M. N. Mulhall, *Contemporary Review*, October, 1881. As rather more than 1,000,000 tons have been added to the Steam-shipping of Great Britain in the three years between 1880 and 1883, the comparison is probably now still more favourable to this country.

to be attributed to the fact that whereas there has been an extraordinary growth in the shipping trade of England since it was liberated from restrictions by the repeal of the Navigation Laws and the adoption of a policy of free trade, the mercantile marine of the United States, under a system of protection, far from showing any increase, is actually declining. As an illustration of this fact it may be mentioned that rather more than twenty years ago 75 to 80 per cent. of the total commerce of the United States was carried in American vessels. The protectionist policy of the United States has received its greatest development since that period, and within that time the mercantile marine of the United States has so diminished that about 80 per cent. of her commerce is now carried in foreign vessels, chiefly English.[1]

It has been well remarked that the American shipping trade has been almost taxed out of existence. No less than twenty different kinds of material which are used in ship-building are taxed under the existing tariff of the United States, whilst the English ship-builder works with untaxed material.[2] The decline in the American shipping trade is

[1] See *Statesman's Year Book* for 1879, 1881, and 1884.

[2] The *Economist* of November 5, 1881, quotes from a well-known American journal, the *New York Commercial Chronicle*, the following list of the taxes imposed by the American tariff on some of the principal materials used in steam-ship manufacture :—

Wrought iron for ships and steam-engines	2c per lb.
Cables and cable chains	2½c ,,
Anchors and parts of anchors	2¼c ,,
Boiler and other plate iron	$25 per ton.
Nails and spikes	1½c per lb.
Cast iron steam pipes	1½c ,,
Rolled or hammered iron	1¼c ,,
Screws for wood	8 to 11c ,,
Sheet iron	1¼ to 3c ,,
Wire, rope, strand, or chain	2c per lb. and 15 per cent.
Wroughts rivets and bolts	2½c per lb.
Wrought steam and water tubes	3½c ,,

the more remarkable when it is remembered that, in order to encourage it, the American people submit to various most harassing restrictions.   Thus, an American citizen is prohibited by law from purchasing ships built abroad to engage in the foreign carrying trade, and is prevented from registering them as American ships even when owned, commanded, and officered by citizens of the United States.

As previously stated, subsidies are given in France not only on the building, but also on the navigation of ships. It is necessary to consider these latter subsidies separately, because they are avowedly granted for reasons very different from those which have induced the French legislature to subsidise the ship-building trade.   As already stated, this particular industry is thus assisted in order to compensate it for the loss which it has to bear in consequence of the existing tariff.   Subsidies are however given on navigation in order to compensate shipowners for " charges imposed on the mercantile navy for the recruitment and service of the military navy."   It would therefore appear that so far as these subsidies only fulfil this object they have no direct bearing on the question of free trade and protection; they obviously however suggest some very weighty considerations which do not come within the scope of this work, as to the effect produced when military and naval regulations are allowed to interfere with industrial progress.

Although the subsidies on navigation are said to be granted for the purpose just described, yet they are so

Steel, in forms not otherwise specified	30 per cent.
Tarred cable and cordage	3c per lb.
Manilla (untarred) cable.	2½c ,,
Other descriptions, untarred	3½c ,,
Sail duck, or canvas, for sails	30 per cent.
Tar and pitch	20 ,,
Planks, deals, and other sawed lumber of hemlock .	$1 per 1,000 ft.
Timber for spars	20 per cent.

arranged as to give an important amount of protection to the French shipping interest. When the Bill which confers these subsidies was passing through the French Senate, an amendment was introduced which makes the navigation subsidy on a French-built ship twice as great as that given on the navigation of a foreign-built ship. The effect of this arrangement is; to increase the subsidy on the building of French ships, for it is obvious that a French merchant, in considering the price which he might be willing to pay for a French or English ship respectively, would take into account the fact that the French ship would be worth so much more in consequence of the more liberal scale on which it would be subsidised. Experience will show to what extent the French ship-building trade may be thus encouraged. From the figures that have already been quoted, it will be seen that the French themselves only expect that their mercantile marine under this fostering care of the State will assume proportions which are insignificant when compared with the mercantile marine of England.[1]

Before leaving the subject it may be well to refer to the fact that such subsidies as those which have just been considered, are sometimes defended on the ground that England gives similar assistance to her shipping trade in the form of postal subsidies. It is however obvious that there is an essential difference between a postal subsidy and one given on the building of a ship. In the case of France it is admitted that the latter is granted to compensate French ship-builders for the extra price they have to pay for materials in consequence of the tariff. A postal subsidy on the other hand is simply a payment made for the conveyance, under certain specified conditions as to

[1] The tonnage of vessels added to the French Mercantile Marine increased from 20,735 in 1881 to 56,594 in 1882; but fell to 35,223 in 1883; a fact which suggests that protection often raises hopes and expectations which it is powerless to fulfil.—M. G. F.

time and speed, of letters, newspapers and other postal
matter.   Such a payment may raise many important questions of administration; thus on the one hand it has been
contended that the State does not receive a service which
is equivalent to the amount paid; and that an equally good
if not an improved conveyance of mails would be secured
if they were treated more as ordinary merchandise.   On the
other hand it has been urged that without some special
arrangement being entered into there are many cases in
which regularity of conveyance would not be ensured, and
that this regularity is so important that the amount paid
in the form of a postal subsidy to secure it, represents
a judicious outlay on the part of the State.   Without
expressing an opinion on the various questions which may
thus be suggested, it is evident that they raise issues very
different from those which are involved in a discussion
as to the relative advantages of free trade and protection.
As a further proof that postal subsidies are not granted
with the object of giving to English shipping any protection against the competition of the shipping of other
countries, it may be mentioned that when a contract for the
conveyance of mails is advertised, no restriction whatever
is imposed upon any foreign vessels competing, and the
subsidy would be paid to foreign-owned and foreign-built
vessels if it were considered that the best and cheapest
conveyance of the mails would thus be secured.   For some
years a subsidy was paid by the English Post Office to a
German steamship company for the conveyance of mails
from Southampton to New York.   In order to show the
different spirit that prevails with regard to postal subsidies
in protectionist countries, reference may be made to the
circumstance that two Bills were recently submitted to the
Congress of the United States with the special object of
assisting through postal subsidies the American shipping
trade, and in order to give this assistance it was proposed
that the postal subsidies should only be paid to vessels

which were built in American ship-yards, and owned and manned by American citizens.[1]

PART II.—*Restraints on Imports.*

In proceeding to consider the effects which are produced by imposing protective duties on imports, it will be necessary in the first instance, to point out the very important difference there is between an import duty which is imposed for purposes of revenue, and one which is maintained with the view of protecting some home industry against foreign competition. A country can obtain a very large portion of its revenue, as England does at the present time, from import duties, without there being a trace of protection in its fiscal system. The import duties which are levied in England may be divided into two classes. First, duties are imposed on articles which are not produced in the country itself, such as tea and coffee; secondly, duties are levied on some article, such as beer or spirits, an excise duty exactly equivalent to this import duty being imposed on English-made beer and spirits. When an import duty only corresponds to an excise duty of the same amount, it is evident that the foreign and the home producer are placed in a position of equality, and the import duty cannot be regarded as protective.

It has been sometimes maintained that even an import duty which comes within the first of these two classes, gives, under certain circumstances, an advantage to the home trader, and thus assumes a protective character. If there are two articles used for similar purposes, and if the one which is imported is taxed, and the other, which is a product of home industry, is untaxed, the import duty undoubtedly would exert a protective influence, because,

---

[1] See Report by Sir E. Thornton, "On the Measures submitted to Congress for Assisting the Shipping Interests of the United States." *Parl. Paper. Commercial.* No. 12. (1881.) (United States.)

by making the article which is imported dearer, it would discourage its use, and would, *pro tanto*, give an advantage to the product of home growth. Thus, if in England when the malt duty. was repealed, no duty had been imposed on beer, and if at the same time an import duty were levied on wine, such a duty might be regarded as protective; because wine which was taxed might often come into direct competition with beer which was untaxed. Such an objection, however, cannot be raised to import duties as they are levied in England. English and foreign-made spirits are taxed at the same rate; and the foreign countries which send us tea, coffee, and wine, cannot complain that these articles are placed at a disadvantage in the English market because they have to compete with English-made beer which is more lightly taxed. The beer duty is certainly quite as high an *ad valorem* tax as the import duty which is levied upon tea and foreign wines. However careful a country may be to remove all traces of protection from its fiscal system, yet it is impossible to prevent an import duty from causing some loss and inconvenience to the countries from which any particular article liable to such a duty is exported. If tea were admitted into England duty free, there would of course be a reduction in its price. The consumption of tea in England would consequently considerably increase; and China, the East Indies and other countries which supply us with tea, would undoubtedly obtain a somewhat better price for tea owing to this increased demand. Although, therefore, all import duties, even if they are not protective, must be disadvantageous to the countries from which the articles are exported which are subjected to duties, yet there is this fundamental and important distinction between an import duty which is imposed for purposes of revenue, and one which is maintained with the object of giving protection to home industry. In the former case, the object those have in view who impose the duty, is to encourage importation; because the greater the importation, the larger is the revenue obtained. In the second case, the object being to discourage importation, the smaller the amount of revenue obtained, the more completely will the purpose of the duty have been achieved. In the entire tariff of the United States there is probably no import duty which is considered to be more entirely' successful than that which is levied on imported copper. This duty so completely defeats foreign competition, that the quantity of copper imported into the United States is quite insignificant. It has even been stated by an eminent American economist that the Government really obtains no revenue at all from the duty, because the 30,000 dols. it yields are supposed to provide a very inadequate compensation for the increased price which the Government pays for the copper used in the navy yards and other State departments.

It is evident that the home trader, independently of any aid that he may derive from protective duties, must always in his own market enjoy an advantage which may be regarded as conferring upon him a kind of natural protection ; because the cost of carriage is necessarily a more important factor in the price of foreign than of home produce. Thus if it cost 30*s*. a ton to send iron from England to Chicago, and only 10*s*. a ton to send it there from the iron districts of Pennsylvania, it is evident that if English iron were admitted duty free into the United States the American ironmasters would still have a great advantage in their own markets. Suppose iron were sold for 5*l*. a ton at Chicago; the English would not be able to obtain one penny a ton more for their iron because of the greater expense to which they had been subjected in bringing it from a greater distance. Consequently of the 5*l*. which the English receive for a ton of iron, only 70*s*. would be paid for the iron : the remaining 30*s*. would represent cost of carriage. The American ironmaster, however, only having to pay 10*s*. a ton for cost of carriage, would receive 90*s*. for each ton of iron which he sold ; he therefore would

virtually obtain 20s. more for every ton of iron than his
English competitor; and this might be sufficient amply to
compensate him for having to pay higher wages or for any
other circumstance which might make the cost of producing
iron in America greater than in England. I have thought it
desirable to describe the advantage which the home trader
thus derives from this natural protection, because it will
be necessary to refer to the subject when considering the
arguments which are advanced in support of protective
tariffs.

In proceeding to consider the effects produced by import
duties imposed for purposes of protection and not for
revenue, it will be important carefully to distinguish between the influence exerted by a protective duty on the
country in which it is imposed, and the influence it exerts
on the countries from which the produce subject to the duty
is exported.

In the introductory chapter allusion was made to the
fact that whereas agricultural produce used to be most carefully protected in England, protective duties are now chiefly
employed in other countries to secure various branches
of manufacturing industry against foreign competition.
Although, therefore, it may appear to be at the present
time of most practical importance to trace the effects of
protecting manufacturing industry, yet there are many
reasons why it is desirable to commence the inquiry by
considering the consequences of imposing protective duties
on the importation of agricultural produce. Manufacturing
and agriculturing industry are so inextricably intertwined
that it is impossible to protect the one without exercising a
considerable influence on the other. Thus it has been
shown that the owners of land on which beet-root is grown
are far more affected by the bounty which is now given in
France on the export of sugar than are the manufacturers
of sugar, although it is their industry which the bounty is
particular intended to foster. A brief description of some

of the consequences which were produced in England by
the protection which was given to agriculture will enable
us more clearly to understand the effects which result from
the protective duties which are now maintained on various
branches of manufacturing industry in France, Germany,
America, and other countries.

It has already been explained that protection may be
regarded as the natural outgrowth of the mercantile system.
Exports were encouraged and imports discouraged with the
primary object of securing a favourable balance of trade.
It was soon, however, perceived that this policy could be
made to serve another purpose; for it was evident that by
thus increasing the foreign demand for any particular product, and imposing difficulties in the way of a supply being
obtained from abroad, a double influence was brought into
operation to raise its price. It used to be almost universally
supposed that to maintain a high level of prices was the
most certain way to secure industrial prosperity. Thus it
was thought that the dearer agricultural produce became,
the more advantageous it would be for farmers, landowners,
and all who were concerned in the cultivation of the land.
Down to 1832 the agricultural interest was able to exercise
a predominant influence in the English legislature; and
consequently agriculture obtained, to a far larger extent
than any other industry, what was then regarded as the
boon of protection. It has already been shown how public
money was spent to procure, through bounties, a high price
for corn in those plentiful seasons when there was a surplus
to be exported; and when seasons were not so favourable,
such effectual precautions were taken to prevent the agricultural interest being deprived of the advantage of high
prices, that Adam Smith tells us that in his time when corn
was below a certain price, its importation was entirely forbidden, and that even in seasons of moderate plenty the
duties on corn amounted to prohibition. With regard to
the importation of other articles of food still greater

solicitude was shown, to secure for the agricultural interest the high prices resulting from a strict monopoly. No live stock and no fresh meat were permitted to be imported; and for many years English farmers and English landowners were so terrified, even at the competition of Ireland, that no Irish cattle were allowed to be sent to England. So mischievous was it considered that the people should use any butter that was not produced in England, that although butter might be imported to serve as grease for machinery, yet the Custom House authorities were strictly enjoined to thrust a stick covered with tar through every firkin of imported butter, and thus render it useless for food. Endless were the ramifications of injustice into which the legislature were led in their desire to protect English agriculture from foreign competition. No sooner was it seen that cotton goods would be largely used than a demand arose that British wool and flax should be protected from such an encroachment.[1] Accordingly, in 1721, a law was passed imposing a penalty of 5*l.* on the wearer, and 20*l.* on the seller, of a piece of calico. Fifteen years later, calicoes manufactured in Great Britain were allowed to be worn, "provided that the warp thereof was made entirely of linen yarn." In 1774, printed calicoes subjected to a duty of 3*d.* a yard, were allowed to be worn. This duty was raised to 3½*d.* in 1806. Raw cotton was at the same time subjected to a heavy import duty. The persistent attempts which were thus made to impede the manufacture of cotton in England afford a striking example of the mischief which a protective policy is liable to produce. It is impossible for the wisest statesman to foresee what will be the course of national industry; from motives of mistaken patriotism, misled by the prevalent theories in favour of protection, English statesmen, for more than a

---

[1] Much interesting information on these and kindred subjects is contained in a book entitled *Cobden and the League*, by the late Mr. Henry Ashworth, of Bolton.

hundred years, for the sake of securing a high price for home-grown wool and flax, put most serious impediments in the way of the progress of the cotton manufacture in this country, which has since become one of the largest and most important of our national industries.

During the closing years of the last, and the commence-· ment of the present century, the foreign trade of England was so much impeded by war, so many ports were closed from which she could have obtained food and other commodities, that prices, especially of agricultural produce, were for many years maintained at an unusually high level. When, therefore, peace was concluded in 1815, the agricultural interest became alarmed. Ports which had been closed were re-opened; prices, it was said, would rapidly fall, and more protection was consequently demanded. The enactments known as the Corn Laws were then passed in deference to the claims thus put forward by those interested in agriculture. The high prices they had obtained in consequence of the war, they now endeavoured to retain through the agency of protective duties. It was therefore enacted that no importation of wheat should be permitted until it had reached the price of 80s. a quarter in the English market, and a proportionately high price was fixed for the exclusion of other grain. These regulations continued in operation, without any material alteration, until 1828, when the sliding scale was introduced. The principle of the sliding scale was to increase the import duties on wheat in proportion to its cheapness in the English market, and thus it was supposed that a high level of prices would be permanently maintained.

When the average price of wheat was			73s.	the duty was	1s.	a quarter
,,	,,	,,	72s.	,,	2s. 8d.	,,
,,	,,	,,	62s.	,,	24s. 8d.	,,
,,	,,	,,	56s.	,,	30s. 8d.	,,
,,	,,	,,	46s.	,,	40s. 8d.	,,
,,	,,	,,	36s.	,,	50s. 8d.	,,

One of the great evils associated with the sliding scale was the extreme uncertainty which it threw over the foreign wheat trade.   Thus if when wheat was at 73s. a quarter in England, a merchant purchased wheat in Odessa at 65s. a quarter, and paid 5s. a quarter for its carriage to England, he might find that, before he could sell it, wheat had fallen in price to 62s. a quarter.   He would not only lose 8s. a quarter owing to this fall in price (this may be considered as the natural and inevitable risk connected with trade), but his loss would be at once quadrupled, owing to the sliding scale ; because, instead of having to pay a nominal duty of 1s. a quarter, he would have to pay a duty of 24s. 8d.   A merchant would not incur this enormous risk, unless he received an adequate compensation.   Wheat consequently would not be imported unless it could be purchased in the foreign market at such a price as would, on the average of transactions, leave a margin sufficient not only to yield the ordinary trade profit and to pay the cost of carriage, but also to provide a fund which might be regarded as an insurance to cover the loss of having to pay a largely increased duty.

After the description which has just been given of the various regulations which, during more than a century, were put in force in England with the object of securing a high price for agricultural produce, it must be admitted that if the welfare of an industry depended upon the protection it enjoyed, those who were engaged in English agriculture ought to have been among the most prosperous of the community.   I will, therefore, proceed to inquire into the influence which was exercised by this protection and by the high prices it produced, upon the three classes concerned in agriculture, namely landowners, farmers, and labourers.   It will be easy to show that these high prices were of no permanent advantage either to farmers or to labourers ; that the extra price which was secured for agricultural produce was appropriated by the landowners in the form of higher rents ;

that neither the profits of the farmer, nor the wages of the labourer, were increased; but, on the contrary, the capital and the labour, which were applied to the cultivation of the land, participated in that general diminution of productiveness with which the entire capital and labour of the country were stricken in consequence of the impediments· which were thrown in the way of the nation's industry. When the Corn Law was passed in 1815, the farmers were confidently told that a beneficent legislature had ordained that wheat would never be less than 80s. a quarter. A glowing description of agricultural prosperity was given, in which the farmers, selling their wheat at 80s. a quarter in all seasons, would be the worthy recipients of increasing wealth which would be largely shared by a happy and thriving peasantry. When the sliding scale was introduced, the farmers were once more told that they had been secured a high price for their corn, and that they could always reckon on obtaining 64s. a quarter for their wheat. During the thirty years between 1815 and 1845, when the corn laws and the sliding scale were in operation, agriculture, instead of enjoying this promised prosperity, was often in a state of exceptional depression. Within this time the causes of agricultural distress were repeatedly the subject of parliamentary inquiry.[1] In a report of a Select Committee, to whom had been referred in 1821 various petitions on the subject of agricultural distress, the following statement occurs: "It is with deep regret that they have to commence their report by stating that in their judgment the complaints of the petitioners are founded in fact, in so far as they represent that at the present price of corn the returns to the occupier of an arable farm, after allowing for the interest of his investment, are by no means adequate to the charges and outgoings, of which a considerable proportion

[1] Committees of the House of Commons inquired into the causes of agricultural distress in the Sessions of 1820, 1821, 1822, and 1836, and a Committee of the House of Lords in 1837.

can be paid only out of the capital and not from the profits
of the tenantry.   This pressure upon the farmer is stated
by some of the witnesses to have materially affected the
retail business of the shopkeepers in country towns connected with the agricultural districts."   From the evidence
given before these committees it was conclusively shown
that the high price of agricultural produce had yielded
no extra profits to the farmer and no extra wages to the
labourer, but that it had been absorbed in increased rents.
In fact the corn laws and the sliding scale, instead of
having conferred any advantage upon the farmers, had
caused them a most serious loss.   The confident opinions
that were expressed at the time the corn laws were passed,
that the price of wheat would be maintained at 80*s*. a
quarter, caused land to be re-valued, and rents to be
re-adjusted on the supposition that farmers would always
sell their corn at this price.   It was soon found that those
who passed these laws had considerably over-estimated the
influence they would exercise on prices, and consequently
the farmers quickly discovered that the chief result to them
of the legislation from which they had expected so much
benefit, was that they had entered into engagements to
cultivate land at a rent which they could not possibly afford
to pay.   This fact powerfully contributed to the success of
the free trade agitation in England.   The fate of protection
was inseparably bound up in this country with the corn laws;
and the corn laws were doomed from the moment when the
farmers could be made to see that these laws, instead of increasing their profits and conferring on them advantages
which other men of business did not enjoy, had induced
them unwarily to agree to pay rents which proved their ruin.

In July, 1843, a meeting was held at Colchester in support of the repeal of the corn laws, and a strenuous effort
was made to convert the meeting into an important protectionist demonstration.   The proceedings of that meeting
showed that protection was about to be successfully attacked

in its stronghold, for the farmers who had hitherto been its most devoted advocates, were at length beginning to perceive that whatever protection might have done for others it had not profited them. The greatest importance was at the time attributed to this meeting. All the agricultural associations of Essex had combined to secure a triumph for the protectionist party. The entire county had been canvassed by the leading landowners, and by the rural clergy. On the day of meeting the farmers assembled in such great numbers that it was supposed even by the advocates of free trade that a resolution in favour of protection would be carried by a large majority. As the proceedings went on the opinion of the meeting seems to have been so completely changed, that a resolution was ultimately passed in favour of free trade by a majority of two to one. This result was chiefly brought about by a speech from Mr. Cobden, who in various ways appealed to the farmers honestly to confess whether they had been made more prosperous by protection. He quoted with great effect the evidence which had been given by several Essex farmers before one of the numerous parliamentary committees which had inquired into the causes of agricultural distress. They all agreed in the opinion that rents had been so high since the corn laws and the sliding scale had been in operation, that the farmers had as a body been unable to pay their way, and that they had been steadily diminishing their capital and adding to their arrears of rent.

With this decline in the prosperity of the farmer and with this decrease in the amount of capital which he could afford to employ in the cultivation of the land, it was inevitable that there should be a marked deterioration in the condition of the agricultural labourer. There probably never was a time when the rural labourer was in a more deplorable condition. With the diminution in the farmers' capital the demand for labour decreased. The general trade of the country had become so paralysed that there was no outlet

E

for the unemployed labour which was steadily accumulating
in the rural districts. Wages consequently were reduced
to a minimum; often not more than 7s. or 8s. a week
could be earned, and the greatest distress prevailed in the
rural districts.

In the life of Mr. Cobden, by Mr. John Morley, an interesting account is given of the condition of the rural
labourers when first the anti-corn-law agitation began its
operations. " In Somersetshire," he writes, vol. i. p. 156,
" the budget of a labourer, his wife and five children under
ten years of age was as follows :—Half a bushel of wheat
cost four shillings; for grinding, baking, and barm, sixpence; firing, sixpence; rent, eighteenpence; leaving out
of the total earnings of seven shillings a balance of
sixpence to provide the family with clothing, potatoes, and
all the other necessaries and luxuries of human existence."
In Devonshire the anti-corn-law lecturers found that the
labourers "seldom saw meat or tasted milk; and that
their chief food was a compost of ground barley and
potatoes."

In thus referring to the depressed condition in which the
farmers and their labourers were at the time when the corn
laws and the sliding scale were in operation, it must not be
supposed that there was no other cause besides protection
for this agricultural distress. The old poor law remained
in operation until 1834, and the encouragement it gave to
every form of improvidence powerfully contributed to lower
the condition of the labouring population. Its pauperising
influence was specially felt in the rural districts, and the
miserable state of dependence and poverty to which the
agricultural labourers were reduced, is probably to be attributed quite as much to its agency as to the impediments
which protection caused to industrial prosperity. Again,
with regard to the position of the farmers under protection
it is obvious that their depressed condition, to which
reference has just been made, cannot be fairly considered as

a necessary consequence of the corn laws and of the sliding
scale.   The effect which these restrictions would have in
maintaining the price of corn at a high level, was over-
estimated, and consequently rents were fixed so high as to
prove disastrous to the farmers.   If there had been no
attempt to give protection to agriculture, this excessive rise·
in rents would have been avoided ; yet the fact that rents
were excessive was undoubtedly due to the impossibility of
estimating what would be the effect on the price of corn
which these restrictions on importation would produce.   It
is however abundantly clear that rents were adjusted in
strict accordance with what was supposed would be the
average price of corn.   General economic considerations
would lead to the conclusion that this is the inevitable
course which would be adopted.   If, with an advance in
agricultural prices, rents remained unaltered, the returns
of the farmer would necessarily be largely increased.   The
exceptional profits which he would enjoy would attract
other capitalists. Farms would be eagerly competed for and
rents would rise.   This competition and the rise in rents
would continue until the extra rent paid neutralized any
advantage which had for a time been derived from the rise
in prices.   During the interval which would elapse before
competition would be able to exercise its full influence the
farmers would be enjoying extra profits.   They would consequently be anxious to employ as much labour as possible ;
the demand for labour would increase, and wages would
advance.   But this advance could only be temporary ; the
extra profits which prompted the increased demand for
labour would, as has been shown, be rapidly absorbed in
higher rents ; even if this were not the case the general
competition of the labour market would prevent labour
employed in agriculture receiving an exceptionally high
remuneration ; just in the same way as the competition of
capital seeking employment will prevent the rate of profit
in any particular industry from being abnormally high.

It therefore appears that the effect of producing by protection a rise in the price of agricultural produce is to cause an advance in rents. This rise in price is however powerless permanently to secure either for the farmer or the labourer any exceptional advantages. The remuneration which they respectively receive must ultimately be determined by the general rates of profit and of wages prevailing in other branches of industry. In order therefore to ascertain the ultimate consequences to the farmer and to the agricultural labourer of raising the price of agricultural produce by the imposition of protective duties, it will be necessary to explain the influence which such a rise of prices will exert on the general industrial economy of the country. If by making food and other agricultural produce dearer, the general remuneration of capital and labour is increased, the farmers and their labourers must share the advantage with the rest of the community, and there will be an advance both in agricultural profits and in agricultural wages. If, on the contrary, it can be shown that by making food dearer, every industry is carried on under greater difficulties, and labour and capital become generally less productive, then the farmers and their labourers will not be able to escape the loss caused by this decline in industrial prosperity, and the returns to their capital and labour will be diminished. It can, I think, be conclusively shown that the inevitable consequence of making food dear must be to diminish the productiveness both of labour and capital, and that in all industries including agriculture there will be a decline both in profits and wages. It is not more certain that the returns to industry will be lessened by making food artificially dear, than it is that the efficient working of a machine will be impeded if unnecessary obstacles are thrown in the way of its free movement. Suppose for instance that by restricting importation, bread, butter, cheese and other articles of general consumption were all made forty per cent. dearer; a labourer would find that what he was before able to purchase for 5s. now cost him 7s. In this event one of two things must occur. If his wages are not advanced in consequence of this rise in the price of food, a most serious loss will be inflicted upon him. His wages, though nominally the same as before, are really greatly reduced, for he finds that all that portion of his wages which he spends in procuring food and the other articles which are made artificially dear, has lost a considerable part of its purchasing power. The loss which will be thus inflicted on him will be more serious than that which others will have to bear; but it can be readily shown that the injury which is done to the labourers will spread far and wide over the rest of the community. Consider for instance how the trade of the manufacturer will be affected. If a labourer has to pay 7s. instead of 5s. for food, so much less will be left to him to lay out in clothes and other articles which he is accustomed to purchase. In all the most important manufacturing industries of a country, it is the outlay of the masses of the people which constitutes the chief demand. If they have less to spend there will be a serious falling off in the demand; trade will become depressed, profits will decline, and the injury thus inflicted both on capital and labour will go on accumulating; for with this decline in profits there will be less inducement to invest capital in business; wages will consequently be reduced and the sufferings of the labourer will be aggravated, for he will find that instead of receiving higher wages to compensate him for the increasing dearness of food, his wages are steadily declining with the diminution of his employer's profits.

In case it should be supposed that this description of the effect of making food artificially dear is merely an imaginary one, deduced from theoretical considerations, it may be well to call attention to some facts illustrative of the general economic condition of England during the thirty years when the corn laws and the sliding scale were in operation, and when the policy of giving protection to agriculture was in its fullest vigour. The period to which I refer was a time of profound peace. That disastrous rivalry in military armaments, which was inaugurated with the establishment of the second empire in France, had not commenced; the national expenditure was at its lowest point; and yet during these thirty years, between 1815 and 1845, there was little development in the trade of the country. In 1841 the exports were about fifty-one millions a year, the precise amount at which they stood a quarter of a century previously. Reference has already been made to the depressed condition of agriculture, and to the fact that during the thirty years that the corn laws were in operation, parliamentary committees were frequently appointed to inquire into the causes of agricultural distress. During the thirty-five years since 1846, agriculture has had no protection; and although there have been times when unpropitious seasons caused losses to farmers, yet on only one occasion has the general condition of agriculture been such as to call for a parliamentary inquiry. But depressed as was the condition of agriculture during the continuance of the corn laws, the general trade of the country was, if possible, in a more unsatisfactory position. The following description is a faithful record, by a contemporary observer, of the condition of the country in 1841, when Sir Robert Peel took office:—"The distress had now so deepened in the manufacturing districts as to render it clearly inevitable that many must die, and a multitude be lowered to a state of sickness and irritability from want of food; while there seemed no chance of any member of the manufacturing classes coming out of the struggle at last with a vestige of property, wherewith to begin the world again. The pressure had long extended beyond the interests first affected; and, when the new ministry came into power, there seemed to be no class that was not threatened with ruin. In Carlisle, the Committee of Inquiry reported that a fourth of the

population was in a state bordering on starvation—actually
certain to die of famine, unless relieved by extraordinary
exertions.   In the woollen districts of Wiltshire the allowance to the independent labourer was not two-thirds of the
minimum in the workhouse." . . . .   "In Stockport, more
than half the master spinners had failed before the close of
1842; dwelling-houses, to the number of 3000, were shut
up : and the occupiers of many hundreds were unable to
pay rates at all.   Five thousand persons were walking the
streets in compulsory idleness; and the Burnley guardians
wrote to the Secretary of State that the distress was far beyond their management; so that a Government Commissioner
and Government funds were sent down without delay."[1]

It is to be particularly noted that the distress which
prevailed at the time was not partial or local, for every
industry was equally depressed.   Those trades which had
for more than a century been most carefully protected,
seem to have been in no single respect in a more satisfactory state than those which had never enjoyed protection.
The legislature had, as already explained, again and again
interposed to protect the woollen industry against the competition of cotton goods, and yet in the description which
has just been quoted the woollen trade is specially referred
to as one which was suffering severe depression.   When
impoverishment had spread so widely that tradesmen in the
large towns said "new clothes had become out of the
question among their customers, and they bought only
remnants and patches to mend the old ones,"[2] it was
evident that trades, whether protracted or not, must alike
be involved in a common disaster.   When the general
industrial condition of a country becomes as unsatisfactory
as was that of England at the period just referred to,
protection is quite as powerless to prevent this depression
spreading to any particular trade, as it is to secure in more

[1] Miss Martineau's *History of the Peace*, vol. ii. pp. 520-21.
[2] *Ibid.* p. 521.

prosperous times an exceptional amount of prosperity for the particular industries which may be protected. It has already been shown that if the price of agricultural produce is advanced, the competition of capital seeking employment would prevent the farmers ultimately appropriating to themselves any extra gains. Just in the same way, if the price of woollen goods were increased by imposing protective import duties, it would be impossible for the woollen manufacturers to appropriate the advantages to themselves. Suppose they were obtaining profits of 20 per cent., whereas the profits of cotton manufacturers were only 10 per cent., capital would be attracted to the woollen trade by the prospect of these large profits, competition would gradually force down prices, until the woollen manufacturer obtained no more than the ordinary rate of profit; the extra price which he received for his goods being only sufficient to compensate him for the extra price which he has to pay for wool in consequence of the importation of foreign wool being restricted by protective duties.

It can in a similar way be shown that the competition of the general labour-market renders it impossible for the labourers who are employed in the industries that are protected, to obtain higher wages than those who are employed in the industries which are not protected. Thus, reverting to the example we have just considered, let it be supposed that the price of woollen cloth is so much advanced by protective duties that woollen manufacturers are able for a time to secure an exceptionally high rate of profit, say 20 per cent., and that in consequence of these large profits, the labourers whom they employ obtain higher wages than are earned by those employed in cotton-mills and other branches of manufacturing industry. It is inevitable that the prospect of obtaining these high wages will attract labour to the woollen trade. The supply of labour in this particular trade will consequently steadily accumulate, until at length wages are no higher in this trade than they are in any other branch of industry. Hence it may be concluded that the rise in price which is caused by protection, whether it be in agricultural or in manufacturing industry, cannot enable either a higher rate of profit or a higher rate of wages to be permanently secured in the industries which are protected. However greatly the price of any particular commodity is advanced, either by artificially stimulating its export or impeding its import, the capital and labour which are employed in its production only receive a remuneration, the amount of which is determined by the return which is yielded to the capital and labour employed in the general industry of the country. Profits and wages therefore cannot be raised in any particular industry by protection, unless at the same time an influence is brought into operation to increase the general rate of profit and wages in all other industries. It has, however, been shown that protection must exert an influence of an exactly opposite kind. If food is made dearer by protection the remuneration of labour is diminished, the general trade of the country is unfavourably affected, and profits decline. A similar effect will be produced, although its influence may not be so immediately felt, by artificially raising through protection the price of any manufactured article, such as iron. If iron becomes dearer a tax is imposed upon the labourer whenever he has to purchase an article of hardware. Again, dearer iron means more expensive machinery, and, if machinery is more expensive, manufacturing industry is carried on under more unfavourable conditions, and from the diminished returns which are yielded there will be less to distribute both in wages and profits. The most striking proof, however, of the injury which is done to a trade by artificially raising through protective duties the price of various materials, is afforded by the fact that it is now thought necessary in France to subsidise French shipbuilders in order to compensate them for the additional price they have to pay for the iron, wood, and other

materials which they employ,. in consequence of the protective import duties imposed under the French tariff.[1]

There is one class, and one class only, that can derive
advantage from a high level of prices being maintained
through protection.   When the price of any article is
increased through protection, the pecuniary value of the
land from which this article is produced is proportionally
increased.   If wheat, by protective duties, is made dearer
the owners of the land on which the wheat is grown can
let it at a higher rent; and in the same way those who own
coal and iron mines can obtain a higher premium for
permission to work these mines if coal and iron are made
dearer by the imposition of protective duties on the importation of these minerals.

It may, perhaps, be thought that some doubt is thrown
upon the correctness of this conclusion, because since protection was abolished in England the rent of land, instead of falling, undoubtedly until recently considerably
increased.   It cannot, however, be too carefully borne in
mind that other influences may simultaneously come into
operation which will greatly modify the effects produced by
any economic agency such as free trade or protection.
Thus, as previously remarked, during the period of the corn
laws and the sliding scale, pauperism was greatly encouraged
by the abuses of the old poor law.   The cost of maintaining this pauperism threw such a serious burden on landowners that in many districts the poor-rates absorbed nearly
the whole net produce of the land, and consequently the
increase of rent which was secured through protection was
in many instances a very inadequate equivalent for the

---

[1] It is a rather strange commentary on the policy of France in giving
a bounty to encourage French shipping and ship-building, that in
December 1884 (three years after this bounty had been in operation)
the French government was stated by the *Pall Mall Gazette* of Dec. 27,
1884, to be in negociation with private shipping firms in England for
the purchase of seven transport-ships.—M. G. F.

increasing charge which poor-rates were constantly imposing. On the other hand, a short time before the introduction of free trade the administration of the poor law was greatly improved by the reforms introduced by the new poor law. The growth of population and the wonderful development in the trade of the country have so much increased the demand for food and other products, that agricultural prices have, on the average, been maintained in spite of foreign importations ; consequently through the operation of these and other favourable circumstances the value of land increased. A very competent authority, Mr. James Caird, has shown, in his work on the " Landed Interest," that between the years 1857 and 1875, the gross annual value of land in England rose 21 per cent., in Scotland 26 per cent., and in Ireland 6 per cent.; and he estimates the increase in the capitalized value of the land during this period to be no less than 331,650,000*l*. It is impossible to say what portion of this increase is to be attributed to the operation of free trade. In many instances the land has been rendered more productive by agricultural improvements, and Mr. Caird estimates the amount that was in this period spent on these improvements to be not less than 60,000,000*l*. After, however, making ample allowance for various circumstances, such as the increase of population and the extension of railways, which have contributed to augment the value of land, it cannot I think be denied that a considerable portion of the increase in the value of land above referred to was due to the great effect produced by free trade in increasing the population and in stimulating the general prosperity of the country.

At the period with which the above comparison was made the cycle of unpropitious seasons which have brought about such serious agricultural depression had scarcely commenced. Since 1875 eight bad harvests in succession have caused great losses to farmers, and have necessitated a very considerable reduction of rents. A part of the addition

to the value of the landed property of the country to which
Mr. Caird refers has undoubtedly now been lost. It must
however be remembered that with the return of propitious
seasons the growth of population and the general increase
in the commerce and wealth of the country will again exert
a favourable influence upon the value of land.   In the
remarks which will be made in a subsequent chapter on
industrial depression I shall have occasion again to refer to
the condition of English agriculture, and I think it will be
shown that there is no reason to suppose that it will permanently continue in its present unsatisfactory position.   A
great effect will be undoubtedly produced on the prosperity
of English agriculture if arrangements are made which will
give more security to capital employed in the cultivation of
the land ; its productiveness would also undoubtedly be
largely increased if, by facilitating its transfer through an
alteration in the existing laws of settlement and entail,
additional opportunity were afforded for the cultivation of
land by those who own it.   If it is thought the continuance
of the recent unpropitious seasons warrants any return to
protection, it cannot be too carefully borne in mind that,
as already shown, the most stringent restrictions on the
importation of food were powerless to secure agriculture
against the effects of bad seasons, and that when the corn
laws were in operation, agriculture was often in a far more
depressed condition than at the present time.   Between the
present depression and that which then had to be encountered there is however this essential difference : the losses
which now have to be borne have chiefly fallen upon
farmers and landowners.   Seldom has there been a time
when the condition of the agricultural labourer has been
more satisfactory.   When, however, unfavourable seasons
occurred during the time when the corn laws were in
operation, not only were the agricultural labourers reduced
to a state of the most abject misery, but every section of the
labouring population suffered the most grievous hardships,

and a depression far more severe than any which has been recently experienced affected every branch of industry in the country.

It is not necessary in this place further to consider the injury which is done by protection, because I shall have occasion again to refer to the subject when considering the arguments advanced by the leading protectionists in the United States and other countries. Before, however, proceeding to discuss these arguments it will be desirable to make some remarks on the general theory of free trade, and this will afford an opportunity of considering whether it is wise for England to adhere to her present policy of unrestricted commerce at a time when many other countries are imposing increased restrictions on the importation of her products, or whether it would be better for her by adopting some form of reciprocity to retaliate upon them for the injury they inflict upon her trade.

CHAPTER III.

NOTHING perhaps is so likely to conduce to a just appreciation of the injury which is inflicted by protection, as to
show that the economic advantages which are produced
by free trade are the same, whether the exchange of commodities is between different countries, or between different
parts of the same country. If we inquire what are the
benefits which the people of England, for example, derive
from trading without let or hindrance among themselves, we
at once see that some product can be raised in one locality
which cannot be raised in another, and some commodities
can be produced under much more favourable circumstances, and therefore much more cheaply, in one district
than in another. Even in a country comparatively so small
as England, there are so many varieties of climate and soil
that various fruits and vegetables which flourish in the
south, will scarcely grow at all in the north. Again, the
mineral resources of a country are usually not spread over
its entire area, but are confined to particular localities. In
many English counties, there never has been, and there
probably never will be, a single ton of coal, of copper or
of iron produced. The people, therefore, of each locality
gain two distinct advantages by freely exchanging their
own commodities for those which are produced in other
parts of the country. In the first place, various articles

are thus obtained which could not otherwise be procured; and, in the second place, various other articles are obtained more cheaply than they could be produced in the locality itself. If there were no trade between a county like Kent, which possesses no coal, and the coal-producing counties such as Northumberland or Durham, it is evident that the people of Kent would have to do without coal, and they would be consequently subject to all the inconvenience and loss which would result from being compelled to use some much more expensive fuel, such as wood. The Kentish landowners, who happened to possess land on which timber was grown, might have the value of their property considerably increased by a rise in the price of timber; but the addition thus made to the property of a limited class would be secured at the expense of an incalculable amount of loss and inconvenience inflicted on the community in general.

It may perhaps be urged, that even in the most protectionist countries there is now never so much interference with freedom of trade as that which has just been described, and that the importation of articles is never obstructed which a community is unable to produce for itself. Protection, it may be said, is confined to imposing restrictions upon the importation of articles which come into successful competition with those of home production. It can, however, be easily shown that even this kind of protection would not be permitted, if it were attempted to apply it with the object of imposing restrictions upon the free exchange of commodities, not between different countries, but between different parts of the same country. It is well known that an extensive manufacture of iron was formerly carried on in many English counties, in which now not a single ton of iron is produced. Sussex and Kent once supplied a considerable portion of the iron which was used in the South of England. The old iron railings round St. Paul's churchyard, which were removed only a few years since, were made from iron which was both raised and smelted in Sussex, and the quality of this iron was undoubtedly equal to the very best that is made at the present day. Iron has ceased to be manufactured in Sussex and Kent, not because the supplies of iron ore have been exhausted there, but because the iron industry in these counties has succumbed to the competition of more favoured localities. Wood was used for smelting iron in Sussex and Kent. With the growing scarcity and dearness of wood, it became more and more hopeless for localities where wood had to be used, or coal had to be imported from a distance, to compete in the manufacture of iron with Yorkshire, Staffordshire, Wales and other districts where fuel is cheap and coal and iron are found in close contiguity. In order to prevent the loss of an important branch of local industry, the iron manufacturers in Kent and Sussex might have claimed protection against this competition which they gradually found more impossible to withstand. But if such a claim had been conceded, what would have been the result? The manufacture of iron might still be carried on in these counties, duties sufficiently high being imposed to neutralize the advantages which other districts possessed for the production of iron. The price of iron would thus artificially be greatly increased in Kent and Sussex; and every one in those counties who had to purchase iron, railway companies having to buy rails for their lines, manufacturers having to buy machinery, farmers having to buy implements, householders having to buy grates and other articles of hardware, would all find that the price they had to pay was increased by twenty, thirty or forty per cent. An onerous tax would thus be imposed on the whole community, in order to preserve this particular local industry, and to guard it against outside competition.

The question is at once suggested—Would such an arrangement be a desirable one for the general community, and would they receive an equivalent return for the sacrifice made? With the view of answering this question, let us in the first place consider what would be the exact effect produced on those engaged in the industry thus artificially fostered. These may be divided into three classes. First, there are those who own the land in which the iron ore is found, and from which the material with which it is smelted is obtained. Secondly, there are the lessees of this land, who supply the capital, and who possess the plant necessary for the manufacture of iron. Thirdly, there are the labourers who are employed in mining the ironstone, in smelting and puddling the ore, and who in various other ways assist in the manufacture of iron. With regard to the last two of these classes, it was shown in the previous chapter that the competition of capital seeking a profitable investment, and the competition of labour seeking remunerative employment, effectually prevent any particular branch of industry from permanently yielding either an exceptionally high rate of profit or an exceptionally high rate of wages. Whenever it is seen that in any trade an abnormally high rate of profit or wages can be obtained, investors and workmen become so anxious to share these special advantages, that increased capital and labour are constantly poured into the trade, until at length the remuneration which it gives both to employers and employed ceases to be greater than that which is yielded in other branches of industry. The capital and labour, therefore, which may happen to be invested in those particular industries which are guarded against foreign competition by protective duties, will only be able to obtain the average or current rate of profit and wages prevailing at the time. If, therefore, the iron trade had through the agency of protection been kept in existence in Sussex and Kent, those who were concerned in the trade, either as employers or employed, would be no better off than those who were engaged in any other of the trades in the locality; the price of iron would no doubt be constantly advancing; but this

F

advance in price would not represent a fund from which a more ample reward could be given to labour and capital; it would, on the contrary, be simply a measure of the increasing difficulties and disadvantages under which the trade was carried on.   As therefore two of the three classes concerned in this trade, the employers and employed, would derive no permanent benefit from its having been preserved, as it were, in a state of unnatural existence, it will be necessary next to inquire whether any advantage would be conferred upon the remaining class of three enumerated, namely, the owners of the land from which the iron is mined, and from which the fuel is obtained with which it is smelted. It is at once evident that they might be considerable gainers, and that the value of their property might be largely increased.   Not only would a rent or royalty be paid for permission to work beds of ironstone, which would remain unworked, and which would consequently have no value at all, if the trade were not preserved through protection, but as timber became more valuable in consequence of the demand for it for smelting purposes, the value of land which was suitable for the growth of timber might be considerably increased.   It therefore appears from the example just investigated, that we are led to the same conclusion at which we arrived in tracing the consequences of protecting home industry against foreign competition, namely that the only class who can derive any permanent advantage from protection are the owners of the land from which are supplied the materials necessary for the carrying on of the particular industry which is protected.   Competition is ever present as an equalising force to prevent capital and labour obtaining a higher remuneration in one industry than in another; and consequently wages and profits cannot continue to be greater in those trades which are protected than in those which are not protected.

In thus attempting to show some of the consequences which would result if free exchange between different parts

of the same country were in any way interfered with, it may
be thought that I have been endeavouring to prove what no
one would now deny.   It may, for instance, be said that the
most ardent protectionist would not now dream of trying
to prevent the free interchange of commodities between
different parts of the same country, and that consequently
he does not require to be convinced of the expediency of
leaving the trade between Kent and Northumberland absolutely unfettered.   If, however, the inexpediency of protecting those who are engaged in some trade in a particular part
of England against the competition of their own countrymen
is self-evident, what reason is there to suppose that restrictions which are admitted to be disastrous if imposed on the
trade between Kent and Northumberland can be less disastrous and, economically, less indefensible, if they interfere
with the free exchange of commodities between Kent and
Normandy?   Exchange of produce between Kent and
Normandy is prompted by just the same motives, and con-
duces to just the same ends, as exchange of produce between
Kent and Northumberland.   Kent would purchase from
Normandy, in precisely the same way as she purchases from
Northumberland, various commodities which she either could
not produce herself, or which could be produced more
cheaply in Normandy.   Normandy, on her part, would
be able to obtain in exchange for the produce she thus
sent to Kent, commodities which she could not produce
herself, or which she could purchase at a cheaper rate from
Kent than she could produce them for herself.

It may be urged that there are social and political considerations which would warrant the imposition of restrictions
upon freedom of exchange between different countries; but
confining our attention for the present to the economic
consequences resulting from such restrictions, I believe it
can be shown that protective duties produce the same effects
whether the industry of any particular locality is protected
against home or against foreign competition.   None of the

circumstances which make it advantageous for trade to be
carried on between Kent and Northumberland, depend upon
the fact that the people of Kent and Northumberland speak
the same language and live under the same government.
If Kent can produce no coal for herself, and if she can only
make iron under such unfavourable conditions as greatly to
augment its cost, it is obviously to her interest to import
coal and iron, and to give in exchange the hops, fruit and
other produce, for the growth of which her soil and climate
give her special advantages.   The benefit which she derives
from this exchange in no way depends upon the coal
and iron which are imported being of home production.
The people of Kent are only interested in getting their
coal and iron where it can be obtained most cheaply and of
the best quality.   Before the last Franco-German war, when
Alsace and Lorraine belonged to France, it was never even
hinted that there ought not to be the most perfect freedom
of trade between these Provinces and the rest of France.
Any proposal to protect a particular branch of French industry against the competition of Alsace and Lorraine, would
have been considered as absurd as a suggestion that if land
on the south bank of the Seine were cheaper than land on
the north bank, the manufacturers in the north of Paris
should be protected against the competition of those who
lived in the south of Paris, because these enjoyed the advantage of having to pay a less price for the ground on
which their manufactories were built.   Unless the annexation of Alsace and Lorraine to Germany has changed the
character of the industries carried on in those Provinces,
how can it possibly be less advantageous for the people of
France to trade with Alsace and Lorraine than it was before
the annexation took place?   If the people of Paris, for instance, used to purchase certain goods from Alsace and
Lorraine, they did so because they thought it was there that
these goods could be obtained on the most favourable
terms; and if they can still be obtained on the same

terms, it cannot be less advantageous now than it was formerly for the people of Paris to continue the trade with
Alsace and Lorraine.   Suppose, however, now that the
annexation has taken place, a duty of twenty per cent. is
imposed upon goods imported from Alsace, in order that
the trade of Germany may be discouraged, and that of
France encouraged.   The inevitable effect of this duty
would be to compel those who purchased these goods to
pay a higher price for them, and consequently an onerous
tax would be imposed upon the general body of the French
consumers of these goods.   But in order fully to appreciate
the injury which the French people would inflict on themselves by pursuing this policy of industrial hostility towards
a neighbouring nation, it should be remembered that not a
single shilling of additional revenue may be yielded to the
State by the taxation which is thus thrown upon them.   Let
it be assumed, for instance, that in consequence of the imposition of this duty, it is found to be more advantageous
to obtain from some other part of France, a certain product
of which 1,000,000*l.* worth had before been annually purchased from Alsace.   The trade, so far as this particular
article is concerned, between France and Alsace, is altogether destroyed.   The price of the product is raised, because it is now obtained under more unfavourable conditions.   This rise in price we may suppose amounts to ten
per cent. ; but as this rise in price may not be sufficient to
compensate the Alsatian manufacturer for the twenty per
cent. duty which he has to pay, he ceases to trade with
France.   It therefore happens that the duty yields no
revenue to the State, although it raises the price of the article
ten per cent., and consequently taxes the French people
just as much as if an income-tax of ten per cent. were imposed on all that part of their income which they expend
in the purchase of this particular article.   The community
receives no equivalent for the sacrifice thus made ; the loss
to the nation is just as real as if, in order to favour the

landowners in some particular district, land in some other
district, which was more fertile than theirs, should not be
cultivated; or as if it were ordered that a country should
not obtain its coal and iron from the most productive
mines; or if it were enacted that manufacturers should not
employ the best and cheapest machinery.

It may, perhaps, be said that although a loss is inflicted
on the French people by their being compelled to pay a
higher price for the articles which had before been obtained
from Alsace, yet a compensating advantage will be secured
through the establishment of a new branch of industry in
France.   But if this were possible, then it would follow that
if, before the annexation of Alsace had taken place, some
particular kind of manufacture which could be most profitably carried on there, had been prohibited, in order
that it might take root in some other part of France, say
Normandy, the French people, although they had to pay a
needlessly high price for an article of general consumption
to encourage the Normandy manufacturers, yet would obtain
a compensation because a new branch of industry had
arisen in that particular part of France.   It is not necessary,
for the moment, to consider what would be the effect on
Alsace; for the point which now has to be determined is
simply this: Is it possible for the rest of France, excluding
Alsace, to be benefited by the establishment in Normandy
of some branch of industry which could be more profitably
carried on in some other locality?   If such a proposal had
been made, would it not have been at once seen that it
would be most unjust to tax the people, for instance, of
Paris, Lyons and Marseilles, by making them pay a higher
price for some article, in order that an industry which
had before thriven in Alsace should now be carried on
in Normandy?   If they had to pay more for this particular
article, they would be able to afford to spend less on other
articles which they might require; and there would be no
reason to suppose that the people of Normandy, where the

new manufacture had arisen, would be better customers of theirs than those by whom the manufacture had previously been carried on. It therefore appears, without taking into account the injury which would be inflicted on Alsace, that no adequate compensation could possibly be obtained by the French people, for the loss which would be inflicted upon them, if industry were, in the manner just described, diverted from its natural channels by compelling some branch of trade to be carried on in a locality where the labour and capital employed in it would not yield the maximum results.

It will perhaps be rejoined, that previous to the annexation of Alsace, no one would have thought of placing any restriction upon the free exchange of commodities between her and the rest of France; because as long as Alsace remained a part of France nothing could warrant her industry being subjected to any special injury; but, it may be said, a policy which could not be defended while Alsace was a French province can be justified as soon as she has been incorporated in the German empire. So long as the Alsatians remained French, anything which lessened their prosperity really tended to lessen the prosperity of France; but when the Alsatians became Germans, any impediment thrown in the way of their prosperity was a disadvantage to Germany, and ceased to be any injury to France. But whatever may be the political advantages which France may consider she secures by impeding the prosperity of Germany, the principle which is here contended for is this : that, viewing the subject only in its economic aspects, the loss which France would have to bear from discouraging some industry which naturally flourishes most in Alsace, is precisely the same whether Alsace is, or is not, a part of France.

If an enumeration is made of the benefits which a country derives from a free interchange of commodities, it will be found that in no single instance does the gain depend upon the two districts, between which the exchange takes place, being parts of the same country. The eastern States of

America find it advantageous freely to trade with the western States, because each produces in abundance some commodity which the other does not produce at all, or because some commodities can be produced at a much less expenditure of capital and labour in one State than in another. But this scarcity and this abundance do not depend upon political circumstances. If, in the American civil war, the North had been defeated, the destruction of the Union would not have brought coal and iron to localities where they are not now to be found. The climate, the soil, would not have been changed. States, the climate of which is too cold for the growth of cotton, would not suddenly have acquired a tropical temperature. It therefore appears that in no single respect does the economic gain which is admitted to result from the free interchange of commodities between different parts of the same country, become in the smallest extent diminished if the districts between which the exchange takes place cease to belong to the same nationality. If it were advantageous that there should be perfect freedom of trade between Alsace and the rest of France, when Alsace constituted a part of the French nation, it cannot be economically less advantageous that there should be the same freedom of trade now that Alsace has been incorporated with Germany. The imposition of commercial restrictions on the trade between France and Alsace may undoubtedly impede the prosperity of Alsace—and thus inflict a loss on Germany; but it cannot be too distinctly borne in mind that it is impossible for this loss to be inflicted on Germany without a loss being at the same time inflicted on France. The injury done to each country is in fact to be exactly measured by the loss which would be caused to the people both of Alsace and of the rest of France, by restricting the Alsatian trade, when Alsace still remained a French province. A policy of commercial restriction, therefore, can only be regarded as economically defensible on the supposition that it is advantageous for a country to make a considerable pecuniary sacrifice in order to hinder the prosperity of neighbouring countries. It is evident that if this were the principle on which the commercial relations between different nations were arranged, countries might be regarded as being in a state of perpetual war; for even in a time of peace, although there would be a cessation of military conflict, industrial hostility would not for a moment be suspended.

Enough has now perhaps been said to show the general economic advantages which result from free trade. It is, however, necessary to consider the subject from another point of view, because of the opinion which is now so frequently expressed in England, that although free trade is an excellent thing in the abstract, and great benefits would result if every nation adopted it, yet one-sided free trade is injurious. It seems to be supposed that England acts in a spirit of foolish and Quixotic generosity, if, whilst other countries impose protective duties on her products, she freely opens her ports to their products. A demand is therefore made for "fair trade," and it appears to be considered by those who urge this demand that it would be better for England to relinquish her policy of free trade if other countries will not act towards her in a spirit of greater fairness. The manner in which it is thought this fair trade should be secured has not been very exactly defined. The prevalent idea, however, seems to be that if England retaliated upon protectionist countries by the imposition on their products of reciprocal duties, they would be forced to abandon some at least of the impediments which they now throw in the way of the importation of English goods. It is not necessary to consider the question as one of moral right, for I think it may be at once admitted that if our manufactured goods are kept out, for instance, of the American markets by heavy protective duties, there would be nothing morally unjustifiable in imposing duties with the view of

impeding the importation of American produce. But, however completely our right to carry out such a policy of retaliation may be acknowledged, the important practical question
remains for us to consider : what are the consequences which
such a policy would produce? The protective tariffs which
are maintained by the United States and other countries,
undoubtedly inflict a very serious injury upon our trade ; and
the simple point to be determined is, whether this injury
would be diminished, or whether it would not be most
materially aggravated, if we, in order to avenge ourselves,
imposed protective duties on their produce. If it were
thought expedient to adopt such a policy of retaliation, it
might undoubtedly be most reasonably carried out against
the United States. The greatest harm which is done to
our trade by protection is the loss of free access to the
American market, and the tariff of the United States is far
more protectionist in its character than the tariff of any
other country. This will at once be shown by comparing
the import duties imposed on certain English products
imported into the United States, France, Germany, and
Austria respectively.[1]

	UNITED STATES.	FRANCE.	GERMANY.	AUSTRIA.
Iron (Bar) per cwt. . . .	4s. 8d. to 7s.	2s. 0½d.	3d.	4s. 0¾d.
Copper, in pigs, per cwt. . .	£1 3s. 4d.	Free	Free	Free
Cotton Yarns and thread per cwt. . .	From £2 6s. 8d. and 20% ad val. to £9 6s. 8d. and 20% ad val.	From 6s. 1d. and upwards ad val.	From 6s. 1d. to £1 15s. 7d.	From 6s. 1d. and upwards ad val.
Woollen Yarns per cwt. . . .	From £4 13s. 4d. and 35% ad val. to £11 13s. 4d. and 35% ad val.	From 8s. 2d. to £1 12s. 5d.	From 4s. 0¾d. to 12s. 2d.	From 1s. 6¼d. to 12s. 2d.
Jute Yarns per cwt. . . .	£1 3s. 4d.	From 2s. 0½d. to 4s. 0¾d.	From 1s. 6¼d. to 18s. 3d.	1s. 6¼d.

[1] See Parliamentary Return, No. 322, 27th July, 1882. *Foreign
and Colonial Import Duties*, Part I.

It will be seen from the above figures that by far the highest import duties, which are levied on English goods, are those which are imposed by the tariff of the United States. Not only are the duties in this tariff exceptionally high, but it embraces a far greater number of articles than the tariff of any other country. By the existing tariff of the United States, import duties are imposed on about 1,500 articles; and there is scarcely a single English product which is allowed free access to the American ports. By far the greater number of these duties are protective; for it rarely happens in the United States that an Excise duty is imposed on a home product to counterpoise the duty on the same product when imported. The tariff of the United States undoubtedly inflicts a very serious injury on English trade; and it can be a matter of no surprise that the loss we thus have to bear should be the more keenly resented, because England is so good a customer of the United States, that taking the latest figures of the aggregate amount of her exports, almost three-fifths are purchased by England. In 1882, the value of the exports from the United States was 146,647,000*l.*; and of this entire quantity 88,352,000*l.*[1] was sent to England. So seriously does the tariff of the United States hinder the importation of English goods into America, that whereas the value of the exports from the United States to England is 88,000,000*l.*, English goods are made so unnecessarily dear in the American markets by protectionist duties, that the value of the goods America purchases from us, although it rose in 1880 to 30,000,000*l.*, only averaged about 25,000,000*l.* a year. These figures certainly show that, with regard to the injury which is inflicted on our commerce by the maintenance of protectionist tariffs, we have a much stronger ground of complaint against the United States than we have against any other country. Consequently, in considering whether it would be expedient to impose a duty on some article of American produce, in

[1] *Statesman's Year Book*, 1884.

order to retaliate upon her for the injury which is done to
our trade by her protectionist tariff, the strongest case is
taken that can be adduced, in support of what is called a
policy of reciprocity or fair trade.

It is frequently said by the advocates of reciprocity, that
nothing can be more unjust than to allow various articles of
American manufacture to be sent to England to compete on
equal terms with our manufactures, when we are forbidden
free access to the American market. Whenever trade becomes depressed, great stress is laid upon the injury which
we suffer from foreign competition; and the impression
becomes widely spread that this depression is, at least in
part, brought about by American goods forcing their way
into our markets. But when the statistics of American
trades are examined, it is at once made manifest that the
injury which is thus done to English trade is so infini-
tesimal as scarcely to be worthy of consideration. The
amount of manufactured goods which is sent from America
to England is so extremely small that it could make scarcely
any difference if this particular part of the trade between the
two countries were to cease altogether. Reference is constantly made to the harm which is done to the cotton trade
of Lancashire, and to the hardware trade of Birmingham,
Sheffield, and other towns, by the importation of cotton
goods and of hardware from America. Yet taking the year
1877, and I select this year because these branches of
English trade were then most depressed, the value of the
entire quantity of manufactured iron and steel imported
into England from the United States was only 200,000*l.*,
and the value of the manufactured cotton imported from
the United States to England in 1876 was 451,876*l.* This
importation, small though it is, was exceptionally large. In
the previous year, the value of cotton goods imported from
the United States to England was only 95,000*l.* And in
1877 it was only 163,000*l.*, or about one-third of what it
had been in 1876. The value of the entire quantity of

manufactured cotton imported into England in 1876 was 1,810,759*l*. and in 1877 it fell to 1,764,802*l*. The unreasonableness of supposing that this trifling importation could to any appreciable extent affect the prosperity of the English cotton trade, is at once made apparent when it is remembered that the value of the cotton manufactures, including cotton yarn, exported from England in 1877, amounted to no less than 69,227,973*l*., and although the value of the manufactured cotton imported rose in 1883 to 2,340,464*l*., the value of the English exports of manufactured cotton rose to 76,445,757*l*.[1]

It therefore appears that no influence of any moment could be produced by levying duties, as the advocates of reciprocity propose, on those articles of American manufacture, imported into England, which come into direct competition with our own manufactures. If we desire to retaliate with effect upon America for the injury which by her tariff she inflicts on our commerce, we must levy duties, not on articles which only constitute a few insignificant items of her trade, but on articles which are exported in such large quantities, that, if the demand for them in England were to decline, the effect would be at once widely felt in America. The commodities which we import in by far the largest quantities from America are products which are either used as food, or which supply the raw material of our most important branches of manufacturing industry.

The following table of the exports from the United States to England in 1880, the items of which are con-

[1] It has been pointed out by Mr. Giffen in a letter to the *Times*, Dec. 31, 1884, that a considerable part of what is rightly entered in the tables of imports as manufactures ought, so far as English industry is concerned, to be looked upon as raw material. He estimates that out of 54,000,000*l*. of manufactures thus imported in 1880, "at least 20,000,000*l*. are indispensable as raw material to our own manufactures." If any attempt were made to tax these articles, the result would be to impede and hamper English manufactures.—M. G. F.

densed from a Table prepared by the Board of Trade,[1] clearly shows that the produce which we purchase from the United States consists almost entirely of food stuffs, and the raw material of various manufacturing industries :—

Live Stock	£3,910,000
Bacon and Hams	9,650,000
Beef, Pork, and other Meat	4,381,000
Butter and Cheese	4,756,000
Lard	1,741,000
Wheat	20,177,000
Maize	9,290,000
Wheat-meal and Flour	5,435,000
Other Grain	695,000
Tallow and Stearine	913,000
Oilseed Cake	1,694,000
Cotton, Raw	31,785,000
Tobacco	1,259,000
Other articles, including Fruit, various Oils, Wood, Naphtha, Rosin, Skins, Ore, and Caoutchouc	8,818,000
TOTAL	£104,504,000 [2]

As the total value of the exports from the United States to England was in the year 1880, 107,082,000*l*., it appears that, with the exception of the comparatively trifling amount of 2,578,000*l*., the whole of these exports consisted

[1] See speech by Right Hon. J. Chamberlain, M.P., delivered in the House of Commons, August 12, 1881.   Appendix.   Table XVI.

[2] A later return, similar to the one quoted above, is in course of preparation at the Board of Trade, but is not yet (Jan. 1885) published. Two tables have, however, been supplied to me, through the kindness of Mr. Giffen ; the first shows that of the total export trade of the United States in the year ending June 30th, 1884, 75 per cent. consisted of agricultural, mining and other raw produce, the remaining 15 per cent. only consisting of manufactures ; the second shows that in the year ending June 30th, 1884, the export of domestic produce from the United States to Great Britain amounted to 79,733,000*l*. Of this 74,109,000*l*. consisted of food, raw produce and live animals, and only 5,624,000*l*. of manufactures : in other words, the manufactures exported were 7 per cent., and the food and raw produce 93 per cent. of the whole.—M. G. F.

of the articles of food and raw produce enumerated in the above table.

If, therefore, we desire to make the American people suffer some of the same loss and inconvenience which they inflict on our commerce by the protectionist tariff they now maintain, it would be necessary to impose import duties either on raw cotton, wheat, or on some of the articles of food which are imported in such large quantities from America. It would, no doubt, be possible in this way to do a very serious amount of injury to many of the most important commercial interests in America. It is supposed that one-half of the entire labour and capital of America is employed in agriculture. The prosperity of American agriculture would be materially impeded if, by the imposition of heavy duties, American produce was to any considerable extent shut out from the English markets. But the question at once suggests itself: Could we thus punish America without at the same time punishing ourselves? In endeavouring to answer this question it can, I think, be shown that although great harm would be done to America, we should inflict a much more serious injury upon our own country.

Suppose, for example, that a duty of ten per cent. were levied on American cotton imported into England. This duty would increase the price of cotton in England, and as a consequence the demand for American cotton would somewhat diminish. England would, in fact, be not so good a customer for American cotton as she was before, and this would be undoubtedly a disadvantage to America. But how trifling is any loss which could be caused to America by this falling off in the demand for her cotton, compared with the widespread mischief which would result to England from the imposition of such a duty. Complaints recur at frequent intervals about the depressed condition of the cotton trade in England. It is often said that the home demand for cotton goods is not so great as it was, and that competition is so active that our manufacturers find it more and more difficult to obtain a profitable market in foreign countries. But if an import duty were imposed on raw cotton every-thing that is now regarded as unsatisfactory in our cotton trade must inevitably become more unsatisfactory. The duty, by increasing the price of raw cotton, would make cotton goods dearer, and this would prejudicially affect the home demand. The consequences however to our foreign trade might be much more serious. If competition with our foreign rivals is now found difficult, what chance would there be of successfully competing with them if we had to bear the burden of having to pay a higher price for cotton than that at which it could be purchased by foreign manufac-turers? The Americans, it is said, are beginning to manu-facture cotton goods nearly as cheaply as we can; and they would undoubtedly be able to make them much more cheaply, if we imposed a duty which caused us to pay an unnecessarily high price for raw cotton. The effect of such a duty might be to imperil the prosperity of our own cotton trade; whereas it might at the same time give an important stimulus to the manufacture of cotton in America. With regard therefore to the product which on the average represents in value at least one-third of our entire imports from America, we are precluded from pursuing a policy of retaliation, because any tax which we might impose on cotton would cause America a loss of trifling importance in comparison with the loss which we should inflict on ourselves.

It can in a similar way be shown that whatever harm might be done to America, by impeding the import of any of those articles of food which she sends to us in such large and increasing quantities, would react upon ourselves with redoubled force. Wheat next to cotton is the article which England purchases most largely from America. In 1877 the value of wheat and flour imported into England from America amounted to 15,127,536*l*., and in 1882 it reached the high figure of 25,000,000*l*. The American farmers would no doubt be considerable losers if they

were prevented having a free access to our markets;
but the loss which might be thus caused them scarcely
deserves consideration when compared with the mischief
which would be done to the entire English nation by the
imposition of even a very moderate duty on American
wheat.   Suppose the duty were 2s. 6d. a quarter, the price
of all wheat in the English market, whether of foreign or
home growth, would be raised by an amount nearly equivalent to the duty; this rise in price may certainly be taken
as not less than 2s. a quarter,[1] and consequently the duty
would take from the English people an amount largely in
excess of the revenue yielded to the State.   If one-half of
the entire quantity of wheat consumed in England were
imported from America, the people, in the higher price
which they would have to pay for their bread, would be
just as much taxed, as if not only an import duty were
imposed on foreign wheat, but an equivalent excise duty
were levied on home-grown wheat.   As such an excise duty
would never of course be levied, the first effect of the import
duty would be to give a protection of 2s. a quarter to
English wheat growers.   The additional price which would
be obtained for English wheat could not, as already explained, be permanently retained by the farmer, but would
certainly be sooner or later appropriated by the landowner
in the form of increased rent; or putting it in another form,
the poorest classes would be taxed with the result of

[1] Although it is impossible to define the exact rise in the price of
wheat which would result from the imposition of such a duty, yet it is
certain that the price would be raised by an amount nearly equivalent
to the duty.   Before the duty was imposed the difference in the price
of wheat of the same quality, say in Liverpool and New York, must
be sufficient to pay the cost of carriage of wheat from New York to
Liverpool.   After the duty has been imposed the difference in price
must be sufficient to pay the duty as well as the cost of carriage.   The
imposition of the duty, by restricting the demand for American wheat,
would somewhat lower its price in America, and consequently so far as
this cause operated, the price in England would not be increased to the
full extent of the duty.

enriching the richest.   But this taxation of a first necessary
of life, serious though it would be, does not by any means
represent all the mischief which might be produced by thus
artificially increasing the price of wheat.   As bread became
dearer the general trade of the country would suffer, for
all industry would be carried on under more unfavourable conditions.   Suppose, for instance, that wages were
advanced sufficiently to compensate the labourers for the
rise in the price of bread, this advance would have one of
two effects, either it would diminish profits, and as profits
became reduced there would be less inducement to invest
capital in industry, or if manufacturers attempted to compensate themselves for the higher wages by charging higher
prices for their goods, this advance in prices might seriously
affect the home demand for their goods, and thus tend to
neutralise the advantage the labourer had gained by higher
wages ; it also would place the English manufacturers at a
disadvantage in competing for custom in foreign markets.
If, on the other hand, wages were not advanced sufficiently
to compensate the labourers, then they would have to spend
a greater portion of their wages in purchasing bread, and
they would consequently be able to lay out less money
upon other articles.   This falling off in the demand of by
far the most numerous class in the community would be felt
by almost every trade in the country.   It therefore appears
that it is impossible for us to retaliate upon America for
the injury which she inflicts on us by her protective tariff,
because we cannot punish her without at the same time
punishing ourselves to a far more serious extent.   Although
much is often said about the harm which is done to our
manufacturers by American competition, yet it is conclusively shown by the trade statistics of the two countries that
the manufactures which are imported from America are
so trifling in amount that scarcely any effect at all would be
produced even if their importation was entirely prohibited.
    It will perhaps however be thought that these objections

would not arise if England carried out a policy of retaliation, and imposed reciprocal duties against other protectionist countries.   It may be argued that whenever an article imported from abroad comes into direct competition with articles of the same kind produced at home, the home trader may be fairly protected against this foreign com-petition if the countries from which the imports come maintain against us protectionist tariffs.   But even if our theoretical right to pursue such a policy is admitted, an insurmountable difficulty presents itself, if it is attempted to be carried out.   Whenever there is any decline of industrial activity in this country, complaints are invariably circulated about foreign competition, and the depression of trade is sure to be attributed to the home market being overstocked with foreign goods; it is at the same time said that our merchants find that protective duties exclude them to a large extent from foreign markets.   A few years ago the iron trade was the particular industry which was most depressed, and from the remarks then frequently made on the subject it ap-peared to be generally assumed that this depression had been to a great extent brought about by iron being sent to our market from Belgium and other countries at a cheaper rate than the English ironmasters could afford to make it.   But a comparison of the quantities of iron which England imports and exports, at once shows that foreign competition can have exercised but little influence in creating the depres-sion.   In the year 1877, when the iron trade was most inactive, the entire quantity of iron and steel manufactured and unmanufactured imported into England amounted to only 2,515,034*l.*, whereas the quantity exported was no less than 20,113,915*l.*   These figures at once show that the foreign ironmasters cannot sell us iron at a cheaper rate than we can make it ourselves ; because if they possessed any such advantage in the production of iron they would drive us out of those foreign markets to which they and we have equal access, and they would gradually appropriate to themselves the larger portion of our export trade. But instead of this taking place the entire value of iron and steel exported from Belgium, the country from whose competition it is said that England has so much to dread, amounted in 1877 to only 1,900,000*l.*; or less than one-tenth of the value of iron and steel exported by England during the same year. Hence England has little to fear from Belgium in those foreign markets to which they have equal access. With regard to Belgian iron competing successfully against English iron in our own market, so little reason is there to suppose our trade can be thus injured that the value of the iron exported from Belgium to England in 1877, a year of extreme depression, exceeded by only 210,724*l.* the value of the iron exported from England to Belgium.[1] It therefore appears that the Belgian ironmasters have nearly as much to fear from the competition of England as the English ironmasters have from the competition of Belgium.[2]

Example after example might be repeated similar to the one just described, which would show that the circumstances of England's foreign trade are such, that a policy of retaliation on her part, even if it were desirable, is impracticable. No single case can be brought forward in which English trade suffers to any appreciable extent by foreign products underselling in our own markets the same articles of English manufacture. Even in those industries where there are most complaints about foreign competition, not only will it be almost invariably found that the aggregate quantity which is imported represents a mere fraction of the entire quantity which is produced by the home trade; but

[1] *Statesman's Year Book*, 1879.

[2] The year 1877 was selected for this comparison because it was a year of extreme depression; but a similar comparison for a later year (1882) brings out even more strikingly the groundless nature of the alarm that was a few years ago excited by the competition of Belgium with England in the iron trade; for whereas the export of manufactured iron from Belgium to England in 1882 was 579,000*l.*, the export from England to Belgium in the same year was 515,000*l.*—M. G. F.

it would be erroneous to conclude that this importation, small though it is, displaces goods of an equivalent value from the home market. Take, for instance, the importation of iron and steel. A very great variety of articles which are imported are described under the general category of iron and steel. All sorts of implements, and various kinds of machinery, are included in this description, and as some of these, for example American sewing-machines, are not made in England, they cannot be considered to compete with English trade. In a few cases it has no doubt happened that some branch of English trade has, for a time at least, been injured by foreign goods being freely admitted to our markets. Great stress is laid by the advocates of reciprocity on the injury which was caused to the riband and silk trades of Coventry, Macclesfield and other places by the abolition of the import duties on foreign silks at the time of the French Commercial Treaty. It is alleged that the French have been enabled so much to undersell us in our own markets, that our silk trade has been almost ruined. It will, however, be found, that although French silks are more largely purchased in this country than formerly, yet any superiority which they are supposed to possess over English-made silks does not arise from greater cheapness, but depends rather upon the better taste which is often shown by the French, both with regard to colour and to the selection of designs for patterns. It is also believed that the French climate, and the quality of the water at Lyons and other French towns, provide more favourable conditions for the dyeing of the silk, and the fixing of the colours, than are to be found in England. In such a case, therefore, if the home manufacturer were protected against foreign competition, protection would be virtually given to him, not to secure him against the cheaper labour of his rivals, but to avert, both from employers and employed, the consequences of not taking the requisite trouble to acquire the skill and other qualities which are possessed by their foreign competitors, or of not being provided with equally great natural advantages.   If the English silk manufacturers suffered in consequence of the competition of cheap French labour, there is no reason whatever why the same competition should not make itself felt in the cotton trade and other branches of manufacturing industry; and yet England still holds such undisputed supremacy in the cotton trade, that, whereas the value of the cotton goods which she exported in 1882 was 75,795,000*l.*, the value of the cotton goods exported by France in the same year was only 3,912,000*l.*

But even if it could not be proved as conclusively as I believe it can be, that, so far as our own country is concerned, a policy of reciprocity is impracticable, the most cogent reasons might still be adduced why such a policy should not be adopted.   Suppose that the injury which was done to the iron trade by foreign competition were not as imaginary as it has been shown to be, and that Belgian iron and steel were sent in considerable quantities into the English market.   If an import duty were imposed with the object of checking this importation, the effect of such a duty would be not only to raise the price of the iron imported, but the price of all the iron produced in England would be advanced by an amount nearly equivalent to the duty.   In 1882 the aggregate quantity of iron imported into England was only about one-thirtieth of the quantity produced in England.   But for the sake of argument let it be assumed that the quantity of iron imported is much larger than it is; that after an import duty has been imposed, England imports one-tenth of all the iron which she annually uses.   Under these circumstances it is evident that the duty would have the effect of taking from the general body of the English people, in the form of the increased price which they would be compelled to pay for iron, an amount greatly exceeding that which the duty yields to the state.   Suppose that the home consumption of English-made iron and steel

is 3,000,000 tons a year, and that, according to the assumption we have just made, one-tenth of this, or 300,000 tons,
is imported. If a duty were imposed it has been shown
that the price of iron would be raised by an amount nearly
equivalent to the duty. If the duty were 30s. a ton it may
be assumed that it would raise the price of iron a pound per
ton. The rise in price would probably be greater than this,
but even if it is taken to be as little as one pound a ton, the
English people would be taxed in the higher price which
they would have to pay for iron 3,000,000l. a year, and of
this amount only 45,000l., the amount of duty paid on the
300,000 tons imported, would be yielded to the state. The
remaining 2,550,000l. would be ultimately appropriated by
the lessees and owners of iron mines. The rise in the price
of iron, thus artificially created, might in the first instance
confer an advantage upon those who were concerned in the
manufacture of iron, whether as employers or employed;
but, as already explained, competition would force down
profits and wages to their normal rate, and the benefit would
ultimately accrue to the owners of the mines.

The effect of thus raising the price of iron, in order to
benefit a special limited class, would be widely felt throughout the entire nation. Every one who used an article which
was wholly or partly made of iron, would find the price he
had to pay for it artificially and unnecessarily increased.
The consequence of this rise of price to the general community would be precisely the same as if a tax were imposed
on every article in which iron was used, on ships, machinery,
railway metal, ploughs, harrows, spades, and on a countless
number of articles in domestic use. It is certain that if
one especial trade were thus subsidised at the public expense,
others would promptly come forward to press their claims
for similar consideration. If the English iron trade were
protected against foreign competition, on what ground would
it be possible to deny similar protection to woollen and
cotton manufacturers, to English farmers, and to every

other industry which had to contend with the competition of foreign products? It is scarcely more certain that a falling stone acquires increased momentum than it is that with each fresh step taken in the path of protection a force would be called into activity to compel a further advance on the same path.   If iron for instance were made unnecessarily dear by the imposition of an import duty, not only would farmers and manufacturers be able to urge that one industry should not be singled out for exceptional favour, but they would be able to claim a right to be compensated for the extra burdens imposed on their industry by the increase in the price of iron.   The impossibility it thus appears there would be of confining a policy of reciprocity within any assignable limits probably constitutes the most cogent of all the reasons that can be adduced against its adoption.

Although the system of "fair trade" or reciprocity is frequently advocated as a remedy for industrial depression, I think it will be shown in a chapter that will be devoted to this subject how indefinitely more serious would the depression which has effected English industry have been if the difficulties which had to be encountered had tempted us to make the smallest departure from the principles of free trade.   This depression it will be shown has been felt with greater severity in many protectionist countries than it has been in England.   And although it is due to many causes, some of which free trade is powerless to counteract, yet I believe it can be established, that when a period of industrial depression occurs, its most serious consequences are not more surely mitigated by free trade than they are aggravated by protection.

CHAPTER IV.

AFTER a careful consideration of the arguments which are adduced in support of protection by those who may be regarded as its leading advocates in America, in the Colonies and in various Continental countries, I think it will be admitted that a full and complete statement of their case will be given by arranging the arguments which are now advanced in support of protection under the following thirteen heads. It will be observed that some of these arguments are of a contradictory character. This circumstance is however accounted for by the fact that protection is regarded from different points of view, and supported for different reasons in different countries; and I have been anxious to omit no argument to which importance is attributed by those who defend protection in the various countries in which it is maintained:

1. Protection is desirable, and especially so in a young country, because it secures diversity of industry. A country such as America or Australia, possessing an almost boundless extent of fertile land, has exceptional facilities for the production of raw material. If therefore manufactures are not fostered by protection, labour and capital will be chiefly devoted to agriculture, and the growth of towns will be discouraged.

2. Protection, by encouraging various branches of home

industry, makes a community much less dependent upon foreign countries.

3. The American protectionists assume that in foreign trade the cost of carriage is paid by the exporting country. Raw produce being more bulky than manufactured goods of the same value, is more costly to export. They therefore argue that America would be placed at a disadvantage compared with England if she imported all the manufactured goods she wanted in exchange for raw produce.

4. It is said that the home manufacturer has to pay various taxes which are not levied from his foreign competitor, and therefore if he does not receive some compensation in the form of protection, he must necessarily be placed at a disadvantage.

5. Protection is advantageous to a country because it encourages various branches of home trade, and discourages to the same extent the trade of foreign countries.

6. A protective import duty, it is asserted, is ultimately almost entirely paid by the foreign producer. Consequently protection secures the double advantage of taxing the foreigner and of encouraging home industry.

7. As profits and wages are not higher in protected industries than in those which are not protected, the objection ordinarily urged against protection—that it benefits a special trade at the expense of the general consumer—cannot be fairly maintained.

8. Protection is economically advantageous, because if a country obtains its produce at home instead of importing it, the labour employed in transporting produce from a distance is saved, and this labour is assumed to be unproductive.

9. Protection is represented as conferring great benefit upon the working classes in America, because the wages which are paid in certain industries which enjoy protection in America are higher than the wages in the same industries in free-trade England.

10. Protection would be unjust if only one industry
were protected, because the general public would obtain no
compensation for the increased price they would have to
pay for the product of this particular industry. They however obtain this compensation, if protection is so extended
that the entire industry of the country participates in its·
advantages.

11. Protection has been defended on the ground that
wages being higher in America and in the Colonies than
in England the American and the Colonial traders require
protection in order to place them in a position of equality
with their English competitors.

12. Protection, having been once established, cannot be
abolished without causing great loss to employers and
employed in those trades which have been protected.

13. Protection can be advantageously introduced into a
young country as a temporary expedient, since various
industries which will ultimately prosper without protection
require its aid in the early stages of their existence.

I will now proceed to consider these arguments in the
order in which they have been stated.

1. *It will be observed that in the foregoing enumeration of
the reasons which are advanced in support of protection the
first position has been given to what is known as the " diversity
of industry" argument, because there is no single point on
which so much stress is laid by American and Colonial
protectionists.*

It is contended that a country which has almost inexhaustible supplies of fertile land, considerable portions of
which are still unoccupied, possesses such exceptional
advantages for agriculture that its labour and capital will
be chiefly concentrated on the production of raw produce ;
it is accordingly maintained that although it might be
cheaper, for instance, for America to purchase from foreign
countries various articles of manufacture with this raw
produce instead of making the articles for herself, yet the

gain thus secured would be dearly bought because of the
harm which would be done to America if there were no
variety in the occupations of her people. If scarcely any
industry were carried on except agriculture, many who were
not suited for outdoor work, but who could acquire a skill
which would enable them to excel in some handicraft, might
find it impossible to obtain any employment for which they
were qualified ; there would consequently be a great waste
of industrial power. It is also alleged that the social
development and progress of the country would be most
seriously impeded if the greater part of its population
devoted itself to field work, and lived in scattered settle-
ments ; whereas if manufactures were established people
would become more concentrated, the growth of towns would
be ensured, and in addition to the foreign demand, there
would arise a large home demand for agricultural produce.

It is evident that the whole of this reasoning rests on the
hypothesis that it is impossible for manufacturing industry
to exist in a young country unless it receives the fostering
aid of protection. It can, I believe, be shown that this
hypothesis is not warranted either by theory or by experience. When a country is first settled and is consequently
very sparsely peopled, it possesses no sufficient supply of
labour for the establishment of manufactures on an extensive
scale. Gradually however, as population increases, there
will arise various branches of domestic industry which will
supplement and assist in various ways the labour of those
who are engaged in agriculture. However purely agricultural the industry of a country may be, there must always be
a great deal of work to be done which will provide many
different kinds of employment besides the mere tilling of
land. Houses and other buildings have to be erected,
roads have to be made, agricultural implements and
machinery have to be repaired, and the cost of carriage
will make many articles, especially those of a bulky kind,
so expensive to import that, although labour may be dearer

in a new country, it will be found cheaper to make the articles at home.   The various trades and handicrafts which are thus called into existence will create an increasing demand for skilled labour, and in this way that industrial uniformity about which the protectionists express so much alarm will be avoided.   It has been already explained that . the home trader, even where no protective duties are imposed, enjoys a natural protection so far as the home market is concerned, because he can bring his produce to this market at a much less cost than can his foreign competitors.

Although the desirability of securing diversity of industries is constantly put forward as one of the chief reasons why protection is supported, yet the tariff which is at the present time maintained in the United States affords a conclusive proof that motives of a very different kind must exercise a powerful influence on those who favour protection.   It will be found by referring to this tariff, that protective duties are not solely imposed on manufactures.   No article for instance is subjected to a heavier import duty than timber.   It cannot be supposed that by excluding Canadian and other timber from the American market, and thus making timber dearer than it otherwise would be, the growth of towns will be encouraged, and that a greater amount of suitable employment will be forthcoming for those who possess the skill required in various handicrafts and who are not fitted for rough outdoor work.   Such a duty exercises an influence in exactly the opposite direction : for when the home timber trade is thus artificially encouraged by protection, a greater number of the population are scattered far and wide over the country, employed in cutting timber and bringing it to market.   The most serious objection to be urged against the policy of imposing duties in order to force into an unnatural existence certain branches of industry arises from the fact, that when the aid of such an agency has once been resorted to, its future operation cannot be controlled. Although it may have been intended by those who first introduced protection into the United States, to do nothing more than give a temporary assistance to certain manufacturers in order to enable them to struggle against the difficulties which often beset a new industry, yet the aid which was thus given, far from being temporary, has been continued for nearly a century; and instead of a few products being protected against foreign competition there is scarcely a single article that can be produced in the United States which is not now subjected on importation to a high protective duty. This extension of protection is not due to any accidental circumstances. Fire is not more certain to spread amongst inflammable material than is protection when once sanctioned to embrace a constantly increasing number of industries within its influence. Each new protective duty which is imposed inevitably creates a demand for more protection in other industries. The ironmasters, for example, of the United States may not improbably demand a greater amount of protection, for high as are the protective duties now imposed on imported iron, amounting in some instances to 100 per cent., foreign iron still finds its way in considerable quantities to the American market.[1] In 1874 no less than 3,000,000*l.* worth of iron was imported. Although this importation subsequently declined, it was in 1881 rapidly increasing and amounted in 1882-3 to 8,159,000*l.* This influx of foreign iron, it may be urged, constantly forces down prices, deprives the ironmasters and those whom they employ of a part of the prosperity to which they are fairly entitled when trade is active, and intensifies the depression of adverse times. If a demand for more protection were conceded, the supply of foreign iron in the American market might be greatly curtailed and the price of American iron would be considerably increased. But the

---

[1] The new tariff adopted in the United States in 1883 introduced many slight modifications in detail in the import duties on iron, without, however, effecting any material change in their general character. See Parliamentary Return, *United States Tariff*, No. 110, 1883.—M. G. F.

moment this advance in price occurred a signal would be given to demand more protection in a great number of other industries. Every article which was made of iron would become dearer, and those who had to purchase these articles would find a new burden imposed upon them. The American cotton and woollen manufacturers might fairly say, " It has been scarcely possible for us to hold our own against our foreign competitors, but now that in order to benefit the iron trade the price of iron has been increased, we have to pay more for our machinery; this places us at a disadvantage compared with English, French and other manufacturers; we have consequently a right to demand an increase of protection, in order to compensate us for the advantage which would otherwise be given to our foreign rivals."

In discussing the various arguments which are adduced in support of protection, it will not be sufficient to consider the subject simply in its economic aspects. Thus, as already stated, the social and other benefits which are conferred upon a country by its possessing a diversity of industries are supposed to provide an ample compensation for any economic loss which may be caused by protection. As complaints are constantly made by protectionists that their opponents persistently ignore all the results of protection which are not economic, I shall be careful to consider these results, and I shall be the more anxious to do so because without such consideration the real magnitude of the mischief which is done by protection cannot be adequately understood. There is nothing more calculated to exercise a deteriorating influence upon a country than to encourage its industrial classes to be perpetually looking to the State for assistance. When a nation becomes thoroughly imbued with the doctrines of protection, it seems to display towards competition the same sort of helpless terror as is shown by a timid child terrified by the fancied presence of a ghostly apparition. The statistics of exports and imports are eagerly scanned, and whenever the import of any particular article

is discovered to be on the increase a piteous cry is raised
for more legislative protection against this growing foreign
competition.   Instead of trying to ascertain whether if the
foreign producer is gaining an advantage, it is not being
secured through greater industrial enterprise, recourse is
immediately had to all the political artifices by which any
particular trade interest can bring its influence to bear on
the Government.   The efforts which are thus being constantly made by those engaged in different industries to
secure legislative aid, have probably done more than anything else to encourage that "lobbying" and "wire-pulling" which form such prominent features in the politics
of the United States.   No inconsiderable portion of the
energy of her public men, which should be devoted to
further objects of national importance, is employed in
gaining for some particular trade what is supposed to be
the privilege of a higher protective duty.   This opinion is
forcibly confirmed by an able American economist, Professor
W. G. Sumner, who says—

"This continual law-making about industry has been
prolific of industrial and political mischief.   It has tainted
our political life with log-rolling, presidental wire-pulling,
lobbying, and custom-house politics.   It has been intertwined with currency errors all the way along.   It has
created privileged classes in the free American community,
who were saved from the risks and dangers of business to
which the rest of us are liable.   It has controlled the elec-
tion of congressmen, and put inferior men in office, whose
inferiority has reacted upon the nation in worse and worse
legislation.   Just now we are undergoing a spasm of indignation at official corruption, and we want to reform the civil
service, but there is only one way to accomplish that, and
that is to cut up the whole system which has made the civil
service what it is."[1]

[1] *Lectures on the History of Protection in the United States*, by
Professor W. G. Sumner.

It would therefore seem to be conclusively established that protection may produce social and political consequences even far more mischievous than the economic loss it causes to a country.

In referring to the social and political influence which is exercised by protection, I think it may be well to direct attention to the encouragement it may give to one of the most serious phases of modern socialism. It may be observed that there is a fundamental difference between the schemes of the earlier socialists and the socialism which in Germany and many other countries is now received with most favour. The chief aim of the earlier socialist was by the formation of voluntary associations to effect certain social reforms, and they proposed to attain their object, not by State assistance, but by conforming to certain rules, which they voluntarily imposed upon themselves, as to their mode of life, and as to the distribution of their property. The socialists of the present day, however, chiefly hope to effect their object by State aid. Whenever a programme of socialism is now put forward, it will be invariably found that a demand is urged for an almost indefinite extension of State intervention. The State is to supply capital to labour. Co-operative associations are to be founded by State loans, the land is to be purchased by the State and relet to the cultivators, and the State is to regulate the number of hours which adults should be permitted to work. This form of socialism has assumed its most marked development in such a protectionist country as Germany, and I think it cannot be doubted that protection must exert an inevitable tendency to foster these socialistic demands for State assistance. If a people are accustomed, as they must be under a system of protection, to believe that the prosperity of each separate branch of industry depends not so much upon individual energy and skill as upon the amount of protection it can obtain from the Government, there can be no surer way of encouraging the growth of a

H

belief not only that industrial prosperity but that the general social well-being of the country is chiefly to be secured not by individual effort but by State help.

2. *The second argument in favour of protection is, that by encouraging various branches of home industry, a community is made much less dependent upon foreign countries.*

This argument may be at once admitted to constitute the only logical basis on which a protective system can be supported; for if it could be assumed that the normal condition of a country was to be perpetually at war with its neighbours, it would become of the first importance to make it, as far as possible, industrially independent of them. Under such circumstances it might be expedient, at whatever cost, to impose protective duties with the view of establishing and maintaining various branches of home industry. It is on grounds such as these that protection is probably most frequently defended. Thus the French consider that they are amply justified in imposing a protective duty on salt, because without such a duty no salt would be produced in France, and all the salt which the French people consume would consequently have to be imported. It is said that in time of war, the coast of France and her frontiers might be so effectually blockaded that no salt could be imported; time would be required to create the necessary appliances for its manufacture: her people might thus be deprived of the supplies they required of a first necessary of life, and they would be placed at a great disadvantage in the war in which they might be engaged. It is therefore maintained that rather than incur this risk it is better for the French people to pay an increased price for the salt which they consume. Let us however endeavour to estimate the exact degree of risk which France would incur of being deprived of its supplies of salt if it were freely imported, and then we shall be better able to judge whether the price which is now paid to avert this supposed danger can be regarded as a wise and judicious expenditure.

It is scarcely possible to imagine any conjuncture of circumstances which would cause France to be engaged in such an universal war that she had not a single ally or a single neutral power on her frontier. The first Napoleon was at one time carrying on war with the greater part of Europe ; and yet there was never a moment even in his unparalleled · career of military aggression, when all the coasts and all the frontiers of France were so completely blockaded that no foreign product could find its way to her markets. There would therefore seem to be every reason to conclude that the danger which protection is supposed to avert is a purely imaginary one. But even if we admit the bare possibility of its occurrence, the question is at once suggested, Cannot some other means be devised of guarding against it, which will prove less burdensome to a country, than compelling its entire people, whether rich or poor, to pay an unnecessarily high price for articles of the first necessity? The consumption of salt in France for domestic purposes may be estimated at about 360,000,000 lbs. Salt is subjected to an excise duty in France of 4s. per cwt. ; but the duty which is imposed on foreign salt when imported being thirty-three per cent. higher than the excise duty, French salt is by this duty so effectually protected that scarcely any salt is imported. It is affirmed on the authority of those who have an intimate practical knowledge of the salt trade that this restriction of foreign importation increases the price of salt in France by a halfpenny a pound ; consequently the protective duty imposes a tax on the French consumers of salt of at least 750,000l. a year, beyond the amount which the duty on salt yields to the French revenue. When it is remembered that salt is used for many purposes in manufacturing and agricultural industry, it is a moderate estimate to assume that the protective duty on salt annually imposes a fine of 1,000,000l. on the French people, beyond the amount which is directly levied from them by the salt tax. This 1,000,000l. a year is taken from them, in order to give

encouragement to the home manufacture of salt, and in
order to make France independent of foreign supplies. It
has also to be borne in mind that the protective duty,
although it imposes this heavy fine on the French people,
far from adding anything to the revenue, actually diminishes
it to a considerable extent. If no protective duty were
imposed on foreign salt, and if the excise and import duty
were exactly the same, the price of salt would be materially
reduced in France : the consumption of salt would consequently be increased, and the revenue would be proportionately augmented, if the import duty were reduced to the
same rate as the present excise. Not only therefore does
protection injure the revenue, but by unnecessarily increasing the price of salt it imposes a tax of at least
1,000,000l. a year on the French people. Not one shilling
of this large amount can be appropriated by the Government
to the general purposes of the State, for it has to be entirely
devoted to compensate the French manufacturers of salt
for the disadvantages under which they carry on their industry, compared with the favourable conditions under which
salt can be produced in England and in other countries.

It is not necessary to express any opinion here with
regard to the expediency of taxing such a necessary of life
as salt. I am simply attempting to trace the effect of pre-
venting the importation of salt by a protective duty ; and
however high the duty imposed on salt might be, it would
cease to be protective if home-made and foreign salt were
taxed at the same rate. From the figures just given an idea
can be formed of the price which is annually paid by the
French people, with the object of guarding themselves
against the remote contingency of a war so universal that
every avenue by which foreign produce could find its way
into France would be completely closed. As such an event
has never yet happened, the greatest alarmist can scarcely
suppose that it will occur more than once in a century. It
would thus appear that in order to provide against it a

contribution amounting in the aggregate to 100,000,000*l.* would be levied from the French people.

If this policy of making a country independent of foreigners is to be carried out, it will not be sufficient simply to protect the home manufacturer of salt against his foreign competitor.   The home production of numerous other articles must be similarly fostered; the price of all these must be artificially raised to such a point as will compensate the home trader for the disadvantages under which he may have to carry on his industry, and thus the loss which is caused to France by making her independent of foreign countries for her supplies of salt may be indefinitely increased.   A most serious burden might in this way be cast upon the entire industry of a nation, and even in periods of profound peace a country would thus be virtually making the most costly preparations for war.   If it were really worth while to take precautionary measures against a danger so shadowy and remote, it would be far cheaper on the eve of hostilities to accumulate stores of the products which are imported, than for a people constantly to have to bear the serious loss which is inflicted on them by articles which they are obliged to purchase being made unnecessarily dear.   When commerce is unhampered by restrictions, the natural action of trade secures on the eve of war the accumulation of stores of commodities the importation of which is likely to be interfered with.   The forces of self-interest would in this way effectually operate without the intervention of the Government.

Although the supposed desirability of making a community independent of foreign countries is one of the arguments most commonly advanced in favour of protection both in America and in our Colonies, yet all the reasons which have been adduced against protection being maintained for this purpose by such a country as France apply with tenfold force to the United States and Canada.   Great as is the improbability that France can ever be cut off from her supplies of foreign products, the improbability is still greater that the United States, Canada, and Australia, with their thousands of miles both of land and sea frontier, could ever be so completely surrounded by hostile forces that they could not continue to obtain supplies from foreign countries.

3. *It is argued in favour of protection, and especially by writers on the subject in America, that the cost of exporting produce being paid by the exporting country, America would be placed at a disadvantage compared with England if the commerce between the two countries consisted chiefly in sending raw produce from America in exchange for manufactured goods; because the former, being in proportion to its value more bulky than the latter, will be more expensive to export.*

It can be readily shown that this argument possesses no validity, for it is based on the erroneous assumption that the cost of exporting produce is paid by the exporting country. In order to prove the fallacy of this assumption, let us inquire what would be the effect of reducing from 6s. to 3s. the cost of sending a quarter of wheat from New York to Liverpool. If, after this reduction in freight took place, American wheat continued to sell in England at the same price as it did before, the profit realized on every quarter of American wheat sold in England would be increased by 3s. This opportunity of securing extra profit would inevitably cause increased supplies of American wheat to be sent to England, and this would continue until the price of American wheat was so much reduced in England that it was not more profitable to sell it there than in America. In the absence of import duties the difference in the price of wheat in New York and in England cannot be permanently greater than the cost of exporting wheat from New York to England. If therefore this cost is reduced, the price of American wheat in England must be also reduced by nearly an equivalent amount. The fall in price would not probably be quite equal to the reduction in the cost of carriage ; because as American wheat became cheaper

in England, the demand for it would become greater, and
this increase in demand might produce a slight rise in its
price in America.   It still, however, is certain that a lessening of the cost of carriage would produce a reduction of
price in the importing country of almost exactly the same
amount, and consequently it follows that the cost of carriage
instead of being borne, as is assumed by American protectionists, by the exporting country, falls almost entirely upon
the importing country.   It is obvious that the first effect of
a rise in the freight between America and England would be
to increase the price, to the English consumer, of wheat
and all other produce imported from America; and any reduction in freights would in the same way confer a greater
advantage upon England than upon America, because the
price of all American produce in the English market would
be reduced by an amount nearly equivalent to the saving
in the cost of carriage.

4. *The next argument advanced in support of protection
is that the home trader needs protection, because, since he has
to pay various taxes which cannot be levied from his foreign
competitors, it is necessary, in order to place him in a position
of equality with them, that he should receive some compensating
advantage.*

With regard to this argument it may be remarked, that
the foreign producer has to pay the taxes which are imposed
in his own country, and it is a mere matter of chance
whether these taxes in the aggregate are heavier than those
that are imposed in the protectionist country.   If protectionists argue that the burdens on production are always
more onerous in a protectionist country, such an admission
may be fairly regarded as a conclusive condemnation of
the protectionist system.   The aggregate amount which has
to be raised by taxation in an old country, such as England,
is in proportion to her population far larger than is required by the Government in the United States.   The
imperial revenue raised in England at the present time

represents a charge of about 2*l*. 10*s*. a head; whereas in
the United States the charge is less than 1*l*. 10*s*. a head.
If therefore the raising of this larger amount in England
proves less burdensome to her industry than the raising of
a smaller amount in protectionist countries, it proves that
their system of taxation is radically defective.

It is also worthy of notice, that if the home trader is to
be protected in proportion to the taxation which he has to
bear, each addition that is made to taxation in a protectionist country will become doubly burdensome to the
general community; because it will create a demand for
fresh protection. Thus if a larger revenue is required in
America, and it becomes necessary to impose a tax on
dwelling-houses and business premises, the American manufacturer would immediately put forward a claim for more
protection. He might, for instance, urge that before this
new taxation he was only just able to compete with his
foreign rivals; the new burdens which he has to bear will
place him at a disadvantage, and he will, therefore, claim
that he should be compensated by heavier import duties
being imposed on the goods which come into competition
with those which he produces. The price of cotton and
woollen goods, of iron, and of various other manufactured
articles, would thus be increased through the imposition of
these higher duties. Consequently the people would be
doubly taxed : they would not only have to provide the
additional revenue which is required, but they would have
to pay a higher price for all those various articles which
were subjected to increased import duties. The increase
of these duties, although extremely burdensome to the
people, might not yield any additional revenue to the
State ; on the contrary, importation would probably be
restricted, and thus the revenue yielded might be less than
it was before.

The argument we are now considering affords a striking
illustration of the mischievous influence which must be

exerted by protection, if a policy of commercial restriction is carried out with logical consistency. The tendency of protection must necessarily be, to deprive the population of the country in which it is maintained, of the advantages arising from any improvements in productive industry which may be introduced into other countries. Thus, if the production of a manufactured article were cheapened in England, so that the English manufacturer was able to sell it in France at a reduction of ten per cent. on its former price, the French manufacturer might not improbably put forward a claim to higher protective duties. It would be in strict accordance with the principles of protection if this claim were granted; and if it were granted the French people would lose the benefit they would otherwise gain in being able to purchase a particular article at a considerably reduced price. In the absence of protection, the home manufacturer who found himself placed at a disadvantage in consequence of his foreign competitor having adopted some improvement, would be stimulated to adopt the same improvement, so as to be able to sell his goods at the same rate as the foreigner. It would thus become a trial of skill against skill, instead of a competition of skill against restriction.

5. *One of the most important advantages claimed for protection by its advocates, is that it not only encourages various branches of home industry, but discourages the trade of foreign countries to a corresponding extent.*

Thus it is argued that if iron were freely imported into the United States, the many millions which are now expended in America in the purchase of iron, instead of being distributed amongst the American manufacturers of iron and their workpeople, would be sent to England. Such a transfer it is assumed would enrich England and impoverish America. It is, however, evident that those who hold this opinion must consider that a community is injured by any circumstance which promotes the prosperity of neighbouring countries. Protectionists may perhaps hesitate to avow such a doctrine when stated in plain terms, but it can be readily shown that this is the conclusion to which the principles they profess inevitably lead.

Protection, as previously remarked, may be regarded as a survival of the mercantile system; the opinions which were propounded by its adherents bear a remarkable resemblance to those which are expressed by the protectionists of the present day. Thus when they insist on the harm which would be done to America if iron were more largely imported from England, they constantly speak as if the additional iron which would be bought from England would have to be paid for in hard cash, and it seems to be thought that America would constantly have more and more money drained away from her. Nothing, however, is more certain than that if America purchased goods more largely from England, the English people would in their turn increase their purchases of American produce. If it were advantageous for a country as far as possible to diminish the quantity of products imported, that country would derive the maximum profit from foreign commerce whose exports were large compared with her imports. To secure a large excess of exports over imports seems in fact to be the goal to reach which protectionists are ever striving. Side by side with the imposition in the United States of innumerable import duties, many of which are so high as to be prohibitive, such eager anxiety is shown that not the slightest impediment should be thrown in the way of foreign countries freely purchasing American produce, that not only is no proposal ever made of levying an export duty in the United States, but the imposition of such a duty is forbidden by the American constitution. Amongst French protectionists the same terror is shown of an excess of imports over exports. Thus in an address of the Chamber of Commerce of Elbœuf, protesting against the renewal of the Commercial Treaty with England, it was stated that whereas in 1875 the exports of France exceeded her imports by 297 million francs, in the next year the imports were in excess of the exports by 271 million francs, and it was said that consequently there had been a transfer in this period of nearly 600 million francs "to the prejudice of France." But if a country is benefited by its exports and injured by its imports, we are led to the conclusion that a community is enriched in exact proportion to the smallness of the return which it receives in exchange for the products which it sends abroad. But if this were the case a community would derive the maximum advantage from foreign commerce when in exchange for various useful products which it exported it received scarcely anything except money. Such a result might no doubt be brought about if a protectionist policy were carried out with sufficient completeness. Suppose for instance that protective duties were increased in the United States; the quantity of articles imported from England and other countries might be greatly diminished, whilst the demand of these countries for American produce would continue. If English harvests, for example, were deficient and America had wheat to spare, this wheat would be gladly purchased by the English people. They would not deprive themselves of bread because America had increased her import duties. If, however, produce continued to be thus exported whilst imports were more and more reduced, a larger portion of these exports would have to be paid for with money, and a larger amount of money would consequently have to be annually transmitted to America. This being the case, the question is at once suggested, would such a transmission of money be more advantageous to America than if, in exchange for the products she exported, she obtained various manufactured goods and other articles which would minister to the wants and enjoyments of her people?

The value of gold and silver is determined by the same laws as those which regulate the value of other articles of mineral produce. If money were constantly poured into a country in the manner just supposed its supply would be increased, and its value would proportionately diminish. Hence, a commerce which consisted in exporting useful products in exchange for money, instead of being peculiarly beneficial would really be specially disastrous to a country ; for produce would be sent abroad which might be used in furnishing the people with the necessaries and enjoy- ments of life ; and in exchange for the real and tangible advantages which were thus parted with, nothing would be secured but an increased supply of money, with a consequent depreciation in its value, producing a rise in general prices.

The policy having been once commenced of creating a "favourable balance of trade" by discouraging imports, could not be continued without imposing more and more onerous and mischievous restrictions on commerce. The rise in general prices which it has been shown would occur in America if she were chiefly paid for her exports with money and not with produce, would obviously tend to diminish the amount of her exports and to increase her imports. If wheat and maize and other articles became dearer in America a less quantity of these articles would be purchased by other countries, and consequently her exports would diminish. At the same time the rise in prices in America might make it profitable for England and other countries to send goods there which before could not be sent except at a loss, and this increase in imports would cause the imposition of higher protective duties to be demanded.

The case which has just been investigated affords another example of the fact that any injury which a country inflicts on the commerce of other nations, instead of yielding her any advantage, is sure sooner or later to react upon herself, and generally with redoubled force. Protectionists, as we have seen, are always most anxious to promote exports and to discourage imports; and yet every new protective duty which is imposed is just as effectual in impeding an export trade as if a duty were levied on every article which is sent abroad. It has, for instance, just been shown that an inevitable result of a protectionist policy is to make the articles which are exported dearer, and consequently to diminish the foreign demand for them. This falling off in the foreign demand will still further be aggravated by the loss which a country inflicts on others besides herself by the maintenance of a protective tariff. England no doubt suffers seriously from the protective duties of America, but the more serious the injury which is thus inflicted on her, and the greater the loss of wealth which it causes, the more will her power of purchasing the goods which America wishes to send her be diminished. If trade improved in England, if employment became more abundant, if profits increased and wages advanced, there is not a single article of general consumption for which the demand would not increase; and this increase in demand is just as certain to take place, whether the article is made at home or whether it is imported.

As it is probable that protection derives special encouragement from the erroneous opinions so often entertained as to the real significance to be attributed to what is termed " the balance of trade," the question will be again referred to in the next chapter, in which will be considered the subject of industrial depression. I think it will then be seen that an unfavourable balance of trade need not necessarily indicate that there is anything unsatisfactory in the industrial condition of a country; for the normal condition of English trade is for the imports largely to exceed the exports, and reasons will be adduced to show that this excess may be taken as one of the surest evidences of the remarkable accumulation of the wealth of England in recent times.

6. *It is argued by protectionists that a protective import duty is ultimately almost entirely paid by the foreign producer,*

and it is therefore supposed that protection secures the double advantage of compelling foreign countries to contribute to the home revenue, whilst at the same time encouragement is given for home industry.

This argument is supported with much ingenuity by a well-known American economist, Mr. Francis Bowen.[1] It is contended by him that if America imported 40,000,000*l.* worth of manufactured goods when an import duty of 10 per cent. was levied, and if when this duty was raised to 35 per cent. only 20,000,000*l.* worth of goods were imported, the Government would not only obtain a larger revenue from the smaller importation, but England in consequence of the falling off in the demand for her goods would be compelled to sell them at a lower price. It is therefore urged that the effect of a protective duty is to enable a country to purchase foreign produce at a cheaper rate, and consequently the country which maintains protection is placed in a position to make a better bargain with those from whom this produce is bought. In this reasoning the fact is altogether ignored that although the price which the English may obtain for their goods is somewhat less than it was before the duty was raised, yet this reduction in price is extremely trifling compared with the extent to which the price is raised in the importing country in consequence of the increase of duty; therefore, although those who purchase the article in America may not find its price advanced by the full amount of the increased duty, the advance will yet be sufficient to cause by far the greater part of the duty to fall upon those who consume the article in America, and not upon those who produce it in England.

In order to show this, let it be assumed, following the example given by Mr. Bowen, that 100,000 pieces of woollen cloth, the value of which in England is 1,000,000*l.*, are exported from England to America when the import

[1] See *American Political Economy*, by Francis Bowen, p. 487.

duty is 10 per cent. Suppose the cost of the carriage of this cloth is 1*l*. a piece, and the duty being 10 per cent. will also be 1*l*. a piece. Consequently the price at which the cloth will sell in America will be approximately 12*l*. a piece, because the price must be sufficient to provide a compensation for the cost of carriage and for the duty. If the price was more than sufficient to do this it would be more profitable to sell cloth in America than in England, and the price would be inevitably forced down by those who had cloth to sell being naturally anxious to secure the advantage of this extra profit. If, on the other hand, the difference in the price of cloth in the American and English markets were not sufficient to pay the cost of carriage and the duty, then it would be less profitable to sell English cloth in America than in England, and English manufacturers would consequently refuse to export cloth. When the duty is raised from 10 per cent. to 35 per cent. a piece of cloth which was worth 10*l*. in England would have to be sold in America not at 12*l*. but at 14*l*. 10*s*., because the difference between its price in the two markets must be sufficient to cover the duty as well as the cost of carriage; the cost of carriage is still 1*l*., but the duty, having been raised from 10 per cent. to 35 per cent., is 3*l*. 10*s*. The protectionists however are no doubt right in their contention that with this great increase in the price of English cloth in America there would be a considerable falling off in the American demand. Accepting the hypothesis on which the argument advanced by Mr. Bowen is based, let it be assumed that the importation of English cloth into America is reduced from 100,000 to 50,000 pieces. This diminution in the demand for cloth would undoubtedly affect its price in England, but the reduction in price would inevitably be small when compared with the increase of duty. The price cannot permanently fall below such a point as will make the manufacture of cloth less remunerative than other branches of industry.

It would be an excessive estimate to suppose that a falling off to the extent of one-half in one branch of the foreign demand for English cloth, resulting from an increase of the American protective duties, would cause a reduction in price of 10 per cent. But even if it is assumed that the price is reduced by this amount, a piece of cloth which before was worth 10*l*. in England would now be worth 9*l*., and its price in the American market would be 13*l*. 3*s*. instead of 14*l*. 10*s*.; because the difference in its price in the two markets must be sufficient to pay the cost of carriage, which is 1*l*., and the duty, which is 3*l*. 3*s*., being 35 per cent. on the value of the cloth which is now 9*l*. It therefore appears that although the price of English cloth in America is not advanced by the full amount of the increase of duty, yet the price is raised from 12*l*. to 13*l*. 3*s*.; in fact cloth is made so dear that the American people can only afford to buy half as much from England as they formerly purchased. An injury will no doubt be inflicted on English trade by this falling off in the American demand : it must however be borne in mind that the loss which may be thus caused to a special branch of English industry may bring with it a compensating advantage. Thus it has been assumed that owing to less cloth being exported to America, cloth becomes cheaper in England by 10 per cent. Every one therefore who wishes to purchase English cloth, whether at home or abroad, will be benefited by its being thus made cheaper. With this fall in price, the general demand will increase ; this will inevitably lead to a considerable recovery in the price of cloth, and this circumstance will go far to compensate the English manufacturers for the falling off in the American demand.

It therefore appears that instead of a protective duty being chiefly paid, as American and other protectionists suppose, by foreign countries, such a duty must cause a much more serious loss to the community which imposes it than it causes to those countries who export the produce on which the duty is levied. Thus it has been shown in the foregoing example, that whatever loss might ultimately be caused to the English cloth manufacturers by an increase of the American import duties on cloth, this loss is, so far as the English people are concerned, accompanied by the advantage that they are able to purchase cloth at a somewhat lower price. One special branch of English trade is injured: whereas the general body of English consumers are benefited. In America, however, where the higher protective duty is imposed, exactly the reverse takes place. Whatever effect the increased duty may have upon the American cloth manufacturers, the increase of the duty causes a most serious loss to the American people.

The arguments that are adduced in favour of protection so habitually ignore the interests of the general consumer, that it is of the first importance to remember that in the case just investigated, the increase of the protective duty on cloth would not simply raise the price of imported cloth, but would produce a corresponding advance in the price of all the cloth which was purchased by the American people, whether of home or of foreign manufacture. If, therefore, of the entire quantity of cloth used in America only one-twentieth were imported, the protective duty on cloth would impose a fine on the American people twenty times as large as the amount which the import duty yielded to the revenue. The injury therefore which is done to a foreign country by the imposition of a protective duty, is trifling compared with the injury which the country imposing the duty inflicts on herself.

7. *A striking illustration is afforded of the opposite aspects under which the advantages of protection are represented by its advocates, when it is argued that the general body of consumers cannot be injured by protection, because profits and wages are not higher in the protected industries than in those which are not protected.*

The employment of such an argument is imprudent,

I

because the fallacy which it involves can be readily explained ; whilst the admission it contains, as to the equality
of wages and of profits in protected and unprotected
industries, affords a complete refutation of many of the
arguments on which most reliance is placed by those who
support protection. Such an admission in fact disposes
of a very considerable number of the reasons which are
ordinarily urged in defence of protection. If it is conceded that profits and wages are not higher in trades which
are protected than in those which are not protected, it at
once becomes evident, as we have attempted to show in a
previous chapter, that if commodities are made dearer by
protection, the loss which is thus caused to the consumer of
these commodities is not counterbalanced by any special
advantage being enjoyed by those who supply the capital
and labour requisite to produce them. When the price of
any product is increased through protection, the extra price
does not represent higher profits or wages, but is simply an
equivalent for increased cost of production.

In order to prove the fallacy involved in the argument
that the consumer cannot be injured by protection because
the imposition of a protective duty, in any branch of
industry, does not increase its wages and profits beyond
the average rate, it is only necessary to consider what would
be the effect of again levying in England an import duty on
corn. As previously explained, the inevitable effect of
such a duty would be to raise the price of corn in England.
Less foreign corn would be imported, and more would be
grown on our own soil. This rise however in the price of
corn, as is admitted by the protectionists in the argument
we are now considering, would not increase the profits of
the farmer ; the extra price which he received for his corn
having to be devoted to pay the additional rent which now
would be demanded from him, he would gain nothing ;
but the fact that he is not benefited, would not in the
slightest degree lessen the loss which would be inflicted

on the general body of the consumers; for, in consequence
of the protective duty, every one would find that he had to
pay more for the bread he purchased.

8. *It is alleged that protection must be economically advantageous, because when a country produces commodities for itself
instead of obtaining them from abroad, the labour employed in
transporting them is saved, and this labour is assumed to be
unproductive.*

There is, however, not the slightest foundation for the
assumption that the labour employed in transporting a
commodity is in any degree more unproductive than the
labour which is employed in actually producing it.   The
labour of the ploughman who ploughs the land on which
wheat is grown, is not more useful or essential than is the
labour of those who bring the wheat to the place where it
is required for consumption.   The finest fields of wheat
would be perfectly worthless if the wheat had to be left on
the fields where it grew.   There may be millions of tons of
coal at the pit's mouth, and this coal would be of no more
use than if it had never been dug, unless there is labour
to convey it to the places where it is wanted.

It is supposed that a coal-field extends under the entire
town of Liverpool.   If this is the case, it would be possible
for the people of Liverpool to obtain coal close to their own
doors.   This coal, however, being at a much greater depth
than the coal in other coal-fields in the locality, would
be more expensive to work.   Let it be assumed that the
additional cost of working the coal will be 5*s.* a ton, and
that the cost of carrying coal from the coal-fields which
now supply Liverpool is 2*s.* a ton.   It is obvious that this
cost of carriage would be saved, if the coal immediately
below Liverpool were worked.   But in order to save this
2*s.*, 5*s.* would have to be spent; and therefore the net loss
on each ton of coal used in Liverpool would be 3*s.*

It therefore appears that saving the labour employed
in transporting produce is not necessarily economically

advantageous, for the amount thus saved may be altogether inadequate to the increased cost involved in obtaining a commodity under more unfavourable conditions.

9. *Protection has been represented to the working classes in America as conferring a great benefit upon them, because it is said that wages are higher in the protected industries in America than they are in the same industries in free-trade England.*

Even if the difference in the remuneration of labour in the United States and in England had continued to be as great as it was formerly, it is obvious, after what was stated when considering the seventh argument, that this difference in wages could not have been due to protection. It was shown that protectionists themselves admit that wages are not higher in protected than in unprotected industries ; consequently the greater remuneration which labour obtains in one country than in the other must be due to causes which are independent of protection, and which exert a similar influence upon all employments. A consideration of some of the more prominent features in the economic condition of England and America respectively will at once enable us not only to say what these causes are, but will also show that far from protection increasing the remuneration of labour in the United States, it is gradually depriving labour of so much of its productiveness, as largely to reduce the difference between the remuneration received by the American and the English labourer respectively.

The most striking point of difference in the economic position of England and the United States, is the comparatively small quantity of fertile land which is possessed by the former country in proportion to its population. The quantity of food which is grown in England would be altogether inadequate for the support of its population ; and each year we are becoming more and more dependent upon America to make good this deficiency in our supplies of food. It is calculated that the quantity of wheat annually

consumed in England is about 22,000,000 quarters; the
yield of our own harvest has often been not more than
9,000,000 quarters, and consequently a considerably larger
quantity has to be imported than is produced by our own
soil. The quantity of meat, butter, cheese and other
articles of food which are annually imported from America
is rapidly increasing. It is not, however, only with regard
to food that England has so largely to depend on foreign
countries for the supplies she requires. A great part of the
raw material which is used in many of her most important
manufacturing industries is not obtained from her own soil.
For instance, a very large portion of the wool which is
annually manufactured in England is of foreign growth;
and the English climate not being suited to the production
of silk and cotton, all the raw silk and raw cotton which
she requires must necessarily be imported. So large a
portion of this cotton is obtained from the United States,
that the value of the raw cotton which is imported thence
has in some years amounted to more than 30,000,000*l*. It
therefore appears that the United States, when compared
with England, enjoys the great advantage of possessing a
more abundant and cheaper supply, not only of food, but
also of the products which provide the raw material of
the most important branches of manufacturing industry. It
would seem necessarily to follow that wages and profits
would both be much higher in the United States than in
England. Fertile land is so plentiful in the former country,
that it can be obtained in any quantity for the payment of
almost a nominal sum; whereas those in England who wish
to cultivate land often have to pay in a single year, in rent,
as much as would represent the fee-simple of land of the
same quality in the United States. In the one country the
entire produce of the land may be devoted to remunerate
capital and labour: whereas in the other country a not inconsiderable portion of the produce has to be appropriated
as rent. The amount which an English farmer has to pay

in rent is often equivalent to the entire amount which he expends in wages. Consequently there will be a smaller aggregate sum left to be divided in the form of profits and wages amongst those who have supplied the capital and labour requisite for the cultivation of the land. It therefore appears that a higher rate of profits and wages must be yielded by agriculture in the United States than in England, and as it has been proved that wages and profits in different industries in the same country approximate to equality, it follows that capital and labour ought both to obtain a higher remuneration in the United States than in England. This higher remuneration is due to circumstances which are altogether independent of protection. It can, moreover, be shown that an influence of so exactly an opposite kind is exerted by protection, that at the present time it is imposing on the industrial classes in America a burden, which to a considerable extent is neutralising the advantages conferred upon them by the possession of those great natural resources to which attention has just been directed.

After what has been stated in a previous chapter, the prejudicial effect which must be exercised upon the remuneration of labour by such a protectionist tariff as that which is now maintained in the United States will be readily understood. A protective duty, by making the product on which it is imposed unnecessarily dear, virtually levies a tax from all those who purchase it. When the commodities which are subjected to such a duty are those in general use, the effect of the duty is precisely the same as if an income tax were levied from the entire community. Such a tax cannot be adjusted or equalised as is the case with the income tax in our own country. Small incomes cannot be exempted; for, however poor a man may be, the tax will fall with unerring certainty on all that portion of his income or his wages which is expended in the purchase of those articles which are protected. But this is not the only tax which protection compels a community to pay. When the instruments and the plant of industry are made more costly, the products of that industry necessarily become more expensive. Iron, copper and timber are, as we have seen, all made dearer in the United States by protection. Consequently the machinery which is made of copper and iron becomes more expensive; the cost of building also, in the construction of which iron and timber are used, is increased; and this being the case, those who pay a higher price for this machinery must be compensated by obtaining a higher price for the products which they manufacture; and those who erect the buildings will be able to claim an increased rent, in order that they may be adequately remunerated for the additional cost of their construction.

Protection is thus in a thousand different ways perpetually taxing the American people. There is not one single branch of her industry on which it does not impose a penalty more or less severe. Its influence may be traced far and wide over the country. It increases the cost of the implements by which the land in the far west is tilled; it causes a higher rent to be paid by the poorest artisan lodged in a back street in New York. The burden thus cast upon the industrial classes is so severe as to neutralise to a considerable extent her great natural advantages. Although wages are considerably higher in the United States than in England, much of the advantage which labour should derive from these additional wages is lost in consequence of almost every article in general use being made unnecessarily dear by protective duties. The wages of an American workman are in this way deprived of an important part of their purchasing power, and when trade becomes depressed the effects of industrial depression are from this cause, as will be subsequently shown, most seriously aggravated.

10. *When protection has once been introduced into a country, it is argued that it should embrace as many*

*industries as possible; because if only one industry were
protected, the general public would receive no compensation
for the higher price which they would have to pay for the
product of this particular industry. If, however, protection
embraces the entire industry of the country, each industrial
class is in its turn benefited, and is amply compensated for
the increased dearness of various articles.*

This argument has been enforced with much ingenuity
by M. Alby, a well-known French protectionist. He con-
tends that if the iron interest alone were protected in France,
the policy would be absolutely indefensible, because every
one in France would have to pay more for iron in order to
give an advantage to those engaged in the French iron
trade ; but he urges that this objection is entirely removed
if all industries are equally protected. For instance, if the
cloth trade is protected, the benefit which those engaged in
it are supposed to derive, more than compensates them for
the loss they have to bear in paying an increased price for
iron. It has been shown with great clearness by the late
Professor Cairnes,[1] that it is impossible to extend protection
to all industries in the manner here contemplated ; and even
if such an extension were practicable, the compensation
which it is assumed the community would receive, would
be entirely illusory. It is obvious, in the first place, that
this argument entirely overlooks the interests of the pro-
fessional and other classes who obtain their incomes
otherwise than by trade. A physician with 1000*l.* a year,
or a policeman with 1*l.* a week, would find that almost
everything he purchased was made dearer by protection;
while his income was in no way increased by it.

With regard to the impracticability of extending protection
to all industries, it is only necessary to remark that in many
industries there is no foreign competition, and it is consequently impossible to extend protection to them. For
example, wine is not imported into, France, and wheat is

[1] *Leading Principles of Political Economy*, p. 454, et seq.

not imported into America. An import duty imposed upon
wine in France, or on wheat in America, would therefore
be of no advantage to the French wine-grower, or to the
American farmer. They are consequently precluded from
receiving any compensation for the higher price which they
are compelled to pay for the various articles that are made
dearer through the operation of protective duties.

11. *Protection is defended in America and the Colonies
on the ground that, as wages are higher there than in
England, the American and Colonial traders require protection in order to place them in a position of equality with
their English competitors.*

This claim for protection is evidently based on the
assumption that the amount of wages paid to labourers is
the only element of which account need be taken when
considering the cost of producing a particular article. The
fallacy of such an opinion at once becomes apparent, when
it is remembered that agriculture is the particular branch of
industry in which the difference between the wages paid in
England and those paid in America or Australia is the greatest.
And yet it is in agriculture that America and Australia can
without the slightest protection compete most successfully
against England. The Illinois or Australian farmer has to pay
his labourers at least two or three times as much as is paid by
the Dorsetshire or Wiltshire farmer, and yet wheat can be
produced much more cheaply in Australia or America than
in England. It is therefore obvious that other circumstances, besides the amount of wages which may be paid,
determine the cost at which any particular article can be
produced ; if this were not so, the American farmer would
have a much stronger claim to protection against the cheap
labour of England than the American manufacturer. The
efficiency of labour must manifestly exert quite as much
influence on the cost of production as the amount of wages
which the labourers receive. The great abundance of cheap
fertile land in Australia and America so much promotes the

efficiency or productiveness of the labour employed in its cultivation, that the cost of producing wheat and other agricultural products is much less than in England, where considerably lower wages are paid to farm labourers. Again with regard to mining industry, it is evident that various circumstances, such for instance as the richness of the mineral deposits and their depth from the surface, must exercise a far greater effect upon the cost of production than the wages which may happen to be paid to the miners.   In manufacturing industry also the possibility of one country obtaining raw material at a less cost than another, may more than compensate for the additional expense which may be thrown upon the manufacturers of the former country by the payment of higher wages. With regard to America and Australia, it is to be particularly noted that the great natural resources which they possess must confer upon them many advantages in industrial competition of which there is no probability that they can be deprived. Their almost inexhaustible supplies of fertile land give them advantages such as are possessed by scarcely any other country.   Their mineral resources are so great that if they suffer from foreign competition, it must be through their own want of skill and enterprise.   Even in manufacturing industry, where it is supposed that protection is most needed, it must be remembered, that as England imports large quantities of cotton from America, and of wool from Australia, these countries must with regard to some most important branches of manufacturing industry enjoy the advantage of cheaper raw material.   It is moreover deserving of special remark, that the difference in wages in countries between which there is an extensive migration of labour must constantly diminish.   When emigration has continued for some time, the objections to it are sure gradually to lessen; it becomes much more of a national habit, and the prospect of a comparatively small difference in the remuneration of labour may be sufficient to induce people to leave their own country, if they think they shall be settling amongst friends and relations, which would prove altogether inadequate if they had to seek a new home amongst strangers. This increasing readiness to emigrate must exert an equalising influence on wages, and must cause the difference in wages in the two countries, between which the migration takes place, steadily to diminish.

12. *Another argument against free trade is, that protection having been once established cannot be abolished without causing great loss both to employers and employed in those trades which have been protected.*

It cannot, I think, be doubted that the loss which might be inflicted upon many special trade interests by the abolition of protection constitutes by far the most serious obstacle in the way of the general adoption of free trade. Exaggerated estimates are no doubt formed of the loss which would be actually caused; but however great may be the stimulus which free trade would give to the prosperity of such a country as the United States, it would in my opinion be impossible suddenly to abolish protection without causing considerable loss to the employers and employed in many trades which, through its aid, had been fostered into a kind of unnatural existence. No industrial change, however beneficial, has ever been introduced without causing some loss and inconvenience to certain special classes. The mechanical inventions which have done most to enrich mankind were not brought into general use without causing great loss and suffering to many whose labour they supplanted. Seldom has a class endured more severe hardships than were borne by our handloom weavers, during the years that they carried on a prolonged and hopeless struggle, striving in vain to compete with products which were made by machinery at a far cheaper rate. Even stage-coaches could not be superseded by railways without some individuals being injured by the change. Although the aggregate wealth of the country was enormously increased, yet in certain special cases property which was before of great value became almost worthless. Along the roads which used to be our great thoroughfares, are still to be found the remains of large inns and posting-houses which formerly let for many hundreds a year; but immediately the railways drew away the traffic these inns so entirely lost their custom that they had scarcely any value at all; many of them were pulled down, and others were converted into cottages. Any attempt to oppose the use of a mechanical invention, because of the loss which it may cause to certain individuals, meets with almost universal disapprobation. Nothing, it is maintained can be more unreasonable than to allow the temporary interests of a few to stand in the way of the permanent advantage of the entire nation. If this principle holds good with regard to the benefits conferred upon a nation by the introduction of a mechanical invention, it holds equally true with regard to the still greater benefits which a nation will derive from the adoption of an unrestricted commercial policy.

13. *Protection can be advantageously introduced into a young country as a temporary expedient, since various industries which will ultimately prosper without protection require its aid in the early stages of their existence.*

This argument in favour of protection, which has been reserved to the last for consideration, is deserving of special attention, not only because of the great weight which is attributed to it by the advocates of protection in the Colonies and in the United States, but also because it has obtained a great amount of importance from the support it received from the late Mr. J. S. Mill. In a passage which protectionists at the present day so repeatedly quote that they seem almost to regard it as the charter of their policy, Mr. Mill says:

"The only case in which, on mere principles of political economy, protecting duties can be defensible, is when they are imposed temporarily (especially in a young and rising nation) in hopes of naturalizing a foreign industry, in itself perfectly suitable to the circumstances of the country.   The superiority of one country over another in a branch of production often only arises from having begun it sooner. There may be no inherent advantage on one part, or disadvantage on the other, but only a present superiority of acquired skill and experience.   A country which has this skill and experience yet to acquire may in other respects be better adapted to the production than those which were earlier in the field: and besides, it is a remark of Mr. Rae, that nothing has a greater tendency to promote improvements in any branch of production than its trial under a new set of conditions.   But it cannot be expected that individuals should at their own risk, or rather to their certain loss, introduce a new manufacture, and bear the burden of carrying it on until the producers have been educated up to the level of those with whom the processes are traditional.   A protecting duty, continued for a reasonable time, will sometimes be the least inconvenient mode in which the nation can tax itself for the support of such an experiment.   But the protectionism should be confined to cases in which there is good ground of assurance that the industry which it fosters will after a time be able to dispense with it ; nor should the domestic producers ever be allowed to expect that it will be continued to them beyond the time necessary for a fair trial of what they are capable of accomplishing."[1]

There is no one more ready than I am to recognise the high authority of Mr. Mill as an Economist, and I will at once admit that the arguments which he advances in favour of the imposition of protection in a young country would be conclusive if there were a reasonable probability that the conditions under which he supposes that such a protective duty could be imposed would ever be realized.   It will be observed in the passage above quoted that he is

[1] See *Principles of Political Economy*, by J. S. Mill, fifth edition, vol. ii. p. 525.

most careful to explain that protection can only be justified as a temporary expedient; and every word which he says in support of protection rests on the supposition, that when an industry has been fairly established the protective duty will be at once voluntarily surrendered by those who are interested in the particular industry. It is, however, incontestably shown by what has happened in the United States and other countries where protection has been long established, that it is absolutely impossible to impose a protective duty under the stipulations on which Mr. Mill so emphatically insists. Whatever professions may be made by those who first ask for protection that it is only required for a limited period, and that it is only needed to enable an industry to tide over the obstacles which may beset its first establishment, it is invariably found that when an industry has once been called into existence through protection, those who are interested in it, whether as employers or employed, instead of showing any willingness as time goes on to surrender protection, cling to the security and aid which they suppose it gives their trade with ever-increasing tenacity. This is shown in a very striking manner by the experience of nearly a hundred years of protection in the United States. In no single instance has a protective duty when once imposed in that country been voluntarily relinquished. Far from any tendency being shown by those who are connected with the industries which enjoy protection to face free competition, they constantly display a feeling of greater dependence, and demand with reiterated urgency additional safeguards against their foreign rivals. A well-known American economist, Professor Sumner, has said: "Instead of strong, independent industries, we have to-day only a hungry and clamorous crowd of 'infants.'" Again, Mr. Wells, with equal force, has remarked: "Although the main argument advanced in the United States in support of protective duties is that their enactment is intended to subserve a temporary purpose, in order

to allow *infant* industries to gain a foothold and a development against foreign competition, there has never been an
instance in the history of the country where the representatives of such industries, who have enjoyed protection for
a long series of years, have been willing to submit to a
reduction of the tariff, or have voluntarily proposed it.
But, on the contrary, their demands for still higher and
higher duties are insatiable and never intermitted." [1]

No amount of theoretical reasoning as to the desirability
of imposing a protective duty as a temporary expedient in
a young country, can outweigh the warnings derived from
experience that no security can be provided against the
permanent continuance of a protective duty when it has
been once imposed. If, after protection has been in operation for nearly a hundred years in the United States, the
various protected interests display a growing determination
to resist any change in the direction of free trade, what
reason is there to suppose that what has happened in
America will not in future years occur in Australia and
other countries, if they should carry out the policy which
now seems to find favour with them, of calling into existence various branches of industry by the imposition of
protective duties?

It is sometimes said that a country may safely adopt a
protective policy, because when the proper time arrived free
trade took the place of protection in England. It has however already been shown that the introduction of free trade
into England was brought about by events so exceptional
in their character, that a protective system when once
established in other countries cannot be assailed with the
same weapons by which its overthrow was effected in England. Agriculture was the industry which, more than any
other, was protected in England against foreign competition.
In all the countries however, such as America, Germany,
France and Australia, in which protection now finds most

[1] *Cobden Club Essays*, second series, 1871, p. 529.

favour, it is chiefly confined to manufacturing industry. These countries either largely export food, or only import it to a limited extent, whereas England is only able to obtain from her own soil a portion of the food which her people require, and consequently is to a great extent dependent upon foreign supplies. When protection, by interfering with the free importation of food, makes food dear, and in a period of national distress deprives the mass of the people of their supply of a first necessary of life, an amount of popular indignation can be excited against the continuance of a system of restriction, which cannot be aroused against it when the results it produces that can be most tangibly brought home to the people, are that it makes various articles of wearing apparel and household furniture dearer. It has been previously shown that an addition to the price of certain articles in general use represents only a very small portion of the mischief which is produced by such a protective system as that which is maintained in the United States. Among other evils which result from protection, it has, for instance, been proved that it places obstacles in the way of the general prosperity of the country; that it exerts an influence in lessening the remuneration obtained by capital and labour; that it discourages industrial enterprise by weakening the feeling of self-reliance; and that it fosters political corruption by inducing various trade interests to use their influence in securing the imposition of duties specially to benefit themselves. These and other evils, inseparably associated with protection, although they inflict an incalculable injury upon a country, are not brought home to the general body of the people with the same distinctness as when, in every humble English home, those who were pinched by hunger could be made to feel that a corn law was in operation which kept from them the food which they so urgently needed.

Nothing can be more unfortunate than if the people of a young country like Australia, who seem to be contemplating an extension of the protective system, should be misled by the example of England and suppose that they would be easily able to return to a policy of free trade whenever the industries, which they hope to call into existence by protection, are once fairly established. England, instead of affording an example to be copied, should furnish rather a warning of that which is to be avoided.   Great as was the injury which protection inflicted on England, there seems every probability that the policy of commercial restriction might have continued in operation for an indefinitely longer period, had it not been for the widespread misery which so frequently recurred in consequence of the restrictions imposed on the importation of corn.   The abolition of the corn laws and the adoption of a policy of complete free trade were undoubtedly hastened by the crisis produced in consequence of the horrors of the Irish famine. So strong was the position of those who were interested in the various monopolies, which had been called into existence in England by protection, that only two or three years before protection was abolished some of the most prominent advocates of free trade in England almost despaired of success.   When it is thus seen that it required such a national catastrophe as the sweeping away of tens of thousands by starvation, to destroy protection in England, the Australian people should feel that if they allow a system of industrial monopoly once to take root in their country, they may have, before it can be got rid of, to pay a penalty not less severe than that paid by the people of our own country before they were able to introduce free trade.

Protection, wherever it is once established, never fails, for reasons previously described, to obtain a firm hold.   There is no reason why protection when introduced into Australia should not in future years become as strongly established as it now is in the United States.   Those who are engaged in all the various industries which are protected, are sure to feel that they are deeply interested in the continuance of the

K

system ; and Australia may experience the same difficulty that is now found in the United States in resisting so powerful a combination of interested opposition.

Enough has now been said to show the extreme peril incurred by any country which adopts a protectionist policy on the plea that it is only resorted to as a temporary expedient. With whatever plausibility such an argument may be advanced, all experience proves that when the paths of restriction have once been entered upon, it becomes increasingly difficult for a nation to retrace her steps. But even if there were any foundation for the opinion of those who apparently believe that protection would be surrendered when the proper time came for its abandonment, I think there is good ground to suppose that the industrial development of a country would be far more surely promoted by freedom than by restriction. Directly the principle is sanctioned that certain special industries are to be fostered by the State, the trade of a country at once ceases to be regulated on purely commercial considerations, and is placed under official and political guidance. The State, in fact, is made the arbiter and superintendent of the entire industrial economy of the country. The State decides what industries shall be called into existence by protection, and determines what is the exact amount of encouragement that shall be given to each particular trade. It is impossible to imagine that any government can be qualified to discharge such functions ; but even if it were qualified to do so, no one can doubt that in determining the exact amount of protection which should be given to particular trades, whether in one instance the duty should be 10 per cent. and in another 20 per cent., the political influence which would be brought to bear by special interests would exercise a far more potent effect than any conclusions which might be arrived at from carefully weighed industrial considerations.

No one who observes what are the most prominent

characteristics in the economic condition of such a recently
settled country as Australia, can doubt that if industry is
there left to its own natural development various trades and
manufactures, which it is sought artificially to stimulate by
protection, are sure gradually to be established without its
aid.   The Australian protectionists say that they want protection in order to enable them to compete against cheap
English labour.   But the remarkable prosperity which is at
the present time enjoyed by their own most important
branch of industry, agriculture, conclusively proves that the
higher wages paid in Australia ought to be regarded as
a measure of the greater natural advantages which she
possesses.   If the mere fact of having to pay higher wages
constituted a claim for protection, the Australian farmer
who has to pay wages three or four times as high as are
generally received by English agricultural labourers, would
not be able to carry on his industry unless he were protected against foreign competition.   It is scarcely necessary,
however, to remark that although very high wages are paid
to farm labourers in Australia, fertile land there is so cheap
and abundant that many agricultural products, such as
wheat and wool, are produced at a cheaper rate in Australia
than they are in England.   Large quantities of these articles
are annually exported from the one country to the other,
and thus it appears that Australia with dearer labour is
able to under-sell England with cheap labour, even in the
English market.

Every circumstance which at the present time impedes
the extension of manufactures in Australia will be certain,
with the progress of the country, to exert less and less
influence, if no commercial restrictions are permitted to
interfere with the free development of her industrial
economy.   The population of Australia is rapidly advancing, and with this advance in population labour will
not only become cheaper, but as its supply increases, there
will be a larger surplus available for employment in other

industries besides those on which her labour and capital are now chiefly concentrated. Moreover, it must be borne in mind that the English people are gradually becoming more accustomed to emigration. They are now much less disinclined than they were formerly to leave their own country. Emigration to Australia was once regarded almost as banishment to a strange and unknown land. English agricultural labourers used to be in such a condition of ignorance and dependence that they went on year after year working for a miserable pittance of 8s. or 9s. a week; they were so deficient in enterprise, and were reduced to a state of such utter helplessness, that they would continue clinging to their own wretched poverty at home, being unwilling or incapable of taking advantage of the prosperous future that was offered to them in other lands. Within the last few years, however, there has been a most remarkable change. The English agricultural labourer, stimulated by various circumstances, such as the spread of education, is rapidly rising from his former condition of torpor and help-lessness; he is beginning to show as much readiness as other labourers to take advantage of any opportunity that may be offered him of improving his condition. It is also to be remembered that each one who emigrates and finds success in his new home, stimulates others to follow in his footsteps. Tidings of the prosperity which he is enjoying are brought to the village which he has left; and a great part of the disinclination which is naturally felt to settling in a new country passes away when it is felt that the new home will be amongst friends and relations, and not entirely amongst strangers.

This increasing readiness on the part of the English labouring population to avail themselves of any opportunity which may be offered to them of improving their condition by settling in a new country, must inevitably cause the remuneration of labour to approximate more nearly to an equality in England, and in the countries which are mainly

peopled by her emigrants.   If therefore matters are allowed
to take their own natural course, any difficulties which may
now impede the establishment of manufacturing industries
in Australia will steadily diminish and ultimately pass away.
On the other hand, if the industrial economy of that country
once becomes involved in the trammels of a widespread
system of protection, every article on which a protective
duty is imposed will be made artificially dear, and the cost
of living will be materially increased.   English labourers
will fail to obtain the advantages from settling in Australia
which they might otherwise enjoy.   Emigration will consequently be checked, and the result of a protectionist policy
must inevitably be to deprive, to a great extent, such a
country as Australia of these additional supplies of labour,
which above all things are essential for the successful
establishment of manufacturing industry.   Australia should
in time be warned by what recently occurred in the United
States.   Reference will in the next chapter be made to the
fact that the difficulties which have to be encountered in
those periods of depressed trade which are certain to occur
are so much aggravated by protection, that in the recent
depression the position of the American workman was so
seriously affected that in the year 1877 nearly as many
labourers left the United States as settled in that country.
At the time, however, when emigration from England to the
United States was thus almost counterbalanced by a flow of
population in the opposite direction, there continued to be
a steady stream of emigration from England to Australia.
In 1877 more than 30,000 persons, of whom a large proportion belonged to the agricultural labouring class, emigrated
from England to Australia, and less than 5,000 returned.
If, however, a policy of protection should once be commenced in Australia, it will surely and rapidly spread.   All
experience shows that it is impossible to confine protection
within narrow and well-defined limits.   If one trade obtains
what is considered to be the benefit of protection, a powerful

inducement is immediately offered to a countless number of other trades to demand that similar privileges should be conferred upon them. With the imposition of each fresh protective duty some article would be made dearer, and thus as the system became generally extended, emigration would be discouraged.

Having now discussed in sufficient detail all the leading arguments that are advanced in support of protection, I will next proceed to consider to what extent the commercial depression which has lately so generally affected industry can be traced on the one hand to the adoption of a policy of free trade, or, on the other hand, to the maintenance of a system of protection.

CHAPTER V.

THE very serious depression which has lately affected the trade of so many countries has given a new interest and vitality to a discussion as to the relative advantages of protection and free trade. This commercial depression produced exactly opposite effects on public opinion in the United States and England. As long as the depression continued, it undoubtedly to some extent lessened the confidence felt in the United States in the efficacy of protection to secure prosperity; while in England, where scarcely any one until lately ventured to utter a dubious word with regard to the benefits conferred by free trade, an inclination is now being shown in many quarters again to lapse into some of the fallacies of protection.

Allusion has been already made to the fact that what is termed "one-sided free trade" has been strongly condemned by some of those who were, until recently, the stoutest defenders of the principles of unrestricted commerce. The opinion certainly seems to be spreading that a country commits an act of foolish self-sacrifice if she persists in opening her markets freely to the products of other countries, when her own products are excluded from foreign markets by protectionist tariffs. This change in public opinion, far from exciting any surprise, may be regarded as the natural result of the manner in which the advocates of free trade and protection respectively have pleaded their cause. Before the commercial depression began, the trade of England had, for a quarter of a century, uninterruptedly advanced with unprecedented rapidity. In the days when we were enjoying this prosperity it used to be perpetually referred to, as affording a conclusive proof of the extraordinary advantages conferred upon a country by free trade. The many other circumstances which have assisted in producing this prosperity were very generally ignored; the statistics of increasing exports and imports were triumphantly appealed to with confidence that nothing more was required for the vindication of free trade, and for the refutation of the doctrines of protection.

Such a mode of considering the subject naturally accustomed people to the idea that the commercial progress of England was wholly due to free trade; consequently many of those who, in prosperous times, were foremost in expressing their approbation of free trade were the first to blame it in a period of commercial depression. The reverse of what occurred in England happened in the United States. For many years the progress in prosperity of the United States was as remarkable as that of England. Although, as I have endeavoured to show, this prosperity was enjoyed, not in consequence, but in spite of protection, it was not unnatural that as long as this prosperity continued, the people of the United States were induced to believe that it was the result of protection. It could be plausibly urged that simultaneously with a great development in her trade and a remarkable increase in her wealth, her tariffs had become more and more protective. Since 1789 the tariff of the United States has been altered no less than forty times, and the tendency of the great majority of these changes has been to make her fiscal system more protective in its character. At the commencement of this period, the import duties imposed averaged about $8\frac{1}{4}$ per cent. with the term of protection limited to seven years; these duties have been steadily increased, until they now are 40, 50, 60, and even, in some instances, 125 per cent.

Nothing consequently could be easier than inseparably to associate, as cause and effect in the popular mind, increased protection and growing prosperity. About the time (1876) that the trade of England became depressed, a still more serious depression fell upon the trade of the United States, and a revulsion of feeling occurred there similar to that which has taken place in England. The people having been in prosperous times taught to believe that the condition of the commerce of their country was far more powerfully influenced by protection than by any other agency, not unnaturally in adverse times singled out protection as the chief cause of commercial depression. So long as prosperity continued, the protectionists in the United States held a position which appeared to be unassailable; and there seemed to be every probability that the tariff would gradually be made more protectionist. The change in opinion, to which reference has been made, was very strikingly shown by a proposal brought forward in 1878, and which met with a considerable amount of support, to carry out in the tariff various important modifications, all in the direction of free trade. Import duties were generally to be reduced to about 25 per cent. Many articles, especially the raw material of various manufacturing industries, were to be admitted duty free, and the number of articles liable to import duties was to be diminished from about 1,500 to little more than 500. Although for a time there seemed to be a probability that this new tariff might be accepted, the return of commercial prosperity has enabled protection to regain its former position in the United States, and there now appears to be little chance that similar proposals in favour of free trade will be revived until the recurrence of another period of commercial depression should bring home to the people of the United States the loss inflicted on them by the system of protection which they now maintain.[1]

[1] The opinion here expressed, that the efforts to promote a lighter tariff in the United States were likely to fail if there was a revival of

It will not be difficult to show that nothing connected with the present commercial depression should cause the English people in the slightest degree to waver in their attachment to the principles of free trade. If commercial depression had only fallen on those countries which maintained a free trade policy, or if the severity of this depression could be shown to be in any way proportionate to the extent to which the commerce of a country was unrestricted, there might be then some justification for the demands which are now in certain quarters made, that we should relinquish our present commercial policy in favour of some form of protection, such for instance as the imposition of reciprocal duties. But however severe may be the depression from which England and other free trade countries have suffered, the depression has certainly been much greater in the United States and in other countries where protective duties are maintained. If the present commercial condition of England is compared with that of the United States, the comparison is to a remarkable extent in favour of the former country. No country in the world has greater or more varied natural resources than the United States. She possesses a boundless extent of fertile land; her supplies of coal, iron, copper and other minerals are practically inexhaustible; her means of internal communication are unsurpassed; within her own boundaries there is almost every variety of climate from the temperate to the tropical, and consequently there is hardly any product that cannot be raised from her soil; and yet with all these natural advantages, although her population exceeds that of Great Britain by more than 40 per cent.,[1] her aggregate foreign trade is only about one-third of the foreign trade of

---

trade, is corroborated by the fact that in 1882-3 the total imports into the U.S.A. were 144,000,000*l.* ; and on these the enormous import duty of 42,706,000*l.* was levied. See *Statesman's Year-Book*, 1884.—M. G. F.

[1] In 1880 the population of the United States was 50,155,783; in 1881 the population of the United Kingdom was 35,003,789.—M. G. F.

England. In 1882 the aggregate exports and imports of the United States were 307,000,000*l*., whereas in the same year the exports and imports of Great Britain were no less than 719,000,000*l*. Throughout the period of commercial depression there was a considerable falling off in the amount of produce imported into the United States. Her imports between 1874 and 1877 fell from 113,000,000*l*. to 90,000,000*l*., representing a reduction of about 20 per cent.[1] During the same period the imports into England, instead of diminishing, slightly increased in value, and consequently the capacity of the English people to pay for foreign produce was not materially affected by the decline in industrial prosperity. There was no doubt a falling oft in the export trade of England, but this decline was by no means so serious as has been sometimes supposed. Between 1860 and 1870 there was an extraordinary increase in the export trade of England. During this period the exports advanced from 164,500,000*l*. to 244,000,000*l*., and when the depression of trade was most severe, the exports from England were 8,000,000*l*. a year more than they were in 1870. It therefore appears that the steady progress of English trade has not been arrested. All that has happened is that her trade has not been maintained at the abnormally high point to which, during two or three years after 1871, it was to a great extent artificially forced, by a speculative demand so unsound that it could not be permanently continued.[2]

In bringing forward the foregoing statistics of the foreign commerce of the United States and England, I do not wish

[1] After 1879 there was a considerable revival in the import trade of the United States, and in 1882 the total imports amounted to 150,000,000*l*. During the same period the imports into the United Kingdom increased from 362,000,000*l*. to 413,000,000*l*.—M. G. F.

[2] English exports reached their lowest point during the recent depression in 1878, when they were 245,000,000*l*. Since that year, however, there has been a rapid increase, and in 1882 they were 306,000,000*l*. —M. G. F.

it to be supposed that I attribute the remarkable difference in the trade of the two countries solely to the fact that the one maintains a protectionist tariff, whereas the other has adopted a free trade policy. As, however, the opinion is so frequently expressed, that the depression from which English industry has suffered is due to free trade, it is well to point out that this depression has fallen far more heavily upon the United States, where protectionist principles are carried out in their most extreme form. Nothing can more conclusively show this than the fact that the advantages offered to labour by the United States, compared with the advantages offered by England, so greatly declined during the period of commercial depression, that in 1877 the number of English labourers who settled in the United States scarcely exceeded the number of those who left the United States for England. However great, therefore, has been the depression of trade in England, it was relatively much greater in the United States. Before the depression commenced, the demand for labour in the United States was so active, and wages were so high, that tens of thousands of labourers were attracted there from England. In the five years from 1869 to 1873, the number of persons emigrating from Great Britain to the United States averaged more than 200,000, and during this time there was scarcely any emigration from the United States either to England or to any other country. During the period of commercial depression, to which we are referring, employment in the United States became so scarce, the falling off in the demand for labour was so much more serious than in England, wages were so much reduced, and at the same time the cost of living was so much increased by the high prices caused by protective duties, that labourers returned in great numbers to England, even at a time when English trade was exceptionally depressed.[1]

[1] The emigration from the United Kingdom to the United States reached its lowest point in 1877, when it amounted to 45,000, and was,

Some hesitation might be felt with regard to the sound-
ness of the principles of free trade, if it could be shown
that in a time when trade was bad the depression falls
least heavily upon those countries whose tariffs are most
protectionist.   What, however, has lately happened is
exactly the reverse of this; for no country maintains
such high protective duties as the United States ; and in
no country has depression been so severely felt, especially
in those very industries which have been most carefully
protected against foreign competition.   The temporary
falling off in the export trade of England is due to a general
decline in the foreign demand, and has not been in the
slightest degree produced by our being driven out of neutral
markets by the competition of protectionist countries.   It
was shown in a previous chapter, that of the exports sent
from America to England, more than nine-tenths consist
of agricultural produce, and the raw material of our manufacturing industries.   A further examination of the export
trade of the United States shows that what is true of her
exports to England, is true of her exports to all the rest of
the world.   The commodities which other countries buy of
her are almost entirely agricultural as distinguished from
manufactured products.   The exports of the United States
consist chiefly of such agricultural products as raw cotton,
wheat, tobacco, meat, &c.   In 1877, out of her entire
exports of 125,500,000l., the following table shows that no
less than 97,300,000l. consisted of such products as those
just mentioned :—

as stated above, nearly counterbalanced by a flow of population in the
other direction. Since 1877, however, the annual emigration from Great
Britain and Ireland to the United States has steadily and rapidly increased. In 1883 it reached the number of 191,573. It may be inferred
that this very rapid increase was in great part due to the disturbed and
distressed state of Ireland, as the total number of emigrants from Ireland
to countries out of Europe rose between 1877 and 1883 from 22,831 to
105,743.—M. G. F.

VALUE OF AGRICULTURAL PRODUCTS EXPORTED FROM UNITED
STATES. 1877.

Cotton, raw	£34,200,000
Wheat and Flour	13,700,000
Corn, Indian	8,300,000
Bacon and Hams	9,900,000
Lard	5,100,000
Cheese	2,500,000
Pork and Beef	2,700,000
Petroleum, refined	11,000,000
Petroleum, crude	700,000
Oilcake	900,000
Tallow	1,500,000
Tobacco, unmanufactured	5,700,000
Hops	400,000
Furs	700,000
	£97,300,000

The exports of agricultural and other raw products from
the United States continue to bear nearly the same proportion to the total export trade, for in 1884 they amounted
to about 138,000,000l. out of an aggregate export of
160,000,000l.

These figures contrast in a very striking manner with
the comparatively trifling value of the manufactures which
are exported from the United States. Much vague alarm
is not unfrequently expressed in England that ruin will
be brought upon our manufacturing industry by American
competition. If a bale of cotton goods or some machine
of American construction is offered for sale in England,
the fact is sure to be carefully chronicled as if it were one
betokening impending disaster to our trade. The following
table, which shows the amount of the chief articles of
manufacture exported by England and the United States
respectively, clearly proves how groundless are the fears that
with regard to manufacturing industry England is being defeated either in her own or in foreign markets by American
competition:—

VALUE OF PRINCIPAL MANUFACTURED ARTICLES EXPORTED FROM ENGLAND AND THE UNITED STATES RESPECTIVELY IN 1877 :—

	ENGLAND.	AMERICA.
Manufactures of Cotton . . .	£69,220,000	£2,040,000
Iron, and manufactures of . .	18,580,000	930,000
Machinery, including steam and other engines, agricultural implements, and, in the case of America, sewing machines .	7,120,000	1,370,000
Linen and Jute Yarn and manufactures.	8,890,000	
Silk Yarn and manufactures. .	2,270,000	
Woollen and Worsted Yarn and manufactures	20,940,000	
TOTAL	£127,020,000	£4,340,000

[1] I leave the table printed above because it refers to 1877, the year of the greatest trade depression ; it will be interesting to compare the figures for 1877 with similar figures for 1882. It will be seen that the increase *per cent.* of American exported manufactures is very considerable ; but, as pointed out by Mr. Giffen, in a letter to the *Times*, this arises mainly from the insignificance of the initial figure.

VALUE OF PRINCIPAL MANUFACTURED ARTICLES EXPORTED FROM ENGLAND AND THE UNITED STATES RESPECTIVELY IN 1882 :—

	ENGLAND.	UNITED STATES.
Manufactures of Cotton	£75,795,000	£2,644,000
Iron, and manufactures of (including telegraph wire)	32,640,000	1,880,000
Machinery, including steam and other engines, rolling stock, agricultural implements, and, in the case of the United States, sewing machines . .	17,571,000	2,754,000
Linen and Jute Yarn and manufactures	9,677,000	
Silk Yarn and manufactures	3,517,000	
Woollen and Worsted Yarn.	22,166,000	
TOTAL	£161,366,000	£7,278,000

M. G. F.

The exports (if any) of the last four commodities from
America are too insignificant to be given in the "Table of
the Principal Articles Exported from the United States."[1]
The figures just enumerated show with striking distinctness
that the recent depression in English trade cannot be in
the slightest degree attributed to American competition.
The export trade of the United States may, on the contrary,
be regarded as conferring on England unmixed benefit.
From the United States we obtain not only the raw material
of many of our most important branches of manufacturing
industry, but we also derive supplies of food, which are
essential to the comfort and well-being of the country.

Reference has already been made to the circumstance
that during the continuance of the recent industrial inactivity, there has been no decline either in the value or the
quantity of the goods imported into England. It therefore
appears that the English people are as large purchasers and
consumers of foreign products as they were before this depression in trade commenced. From this and other facts,
to which reference will presently be made, I think the
conclusion may be fairly drawn that the effect of this depression on the general prosperity of the country has been
very considerably exaggerated; and that although those
engaged, whether as employers or employed, in certain
special trades, have been very seriously affected, yet there
has been nothing in the general condition of the country
to excite apprehension. In the mean time, however, it
may be desirable to direct attention to the fear which
is not unfrequently expressed, that the maintenance
of our import trade, at a time when there is a certain
diminution in exports, is a subject for grave misgiving, and
shows that the seeds of future mischief are being sown
which are certain hereafter to bring disaster upon our
national industry. These fears have their origin in the

[1] See *Statistical Abstract for Principal Foreign Countries*, 1878, 1883,
and 1884.

large excess in the value of the goods which are imported
by England, compared with the value of goods exported.
Taking the figures of the latest year (1883) for which
they are given in the *Statistical Abstract*, issued by the
Board of Trade, it will be seen that this excess amounts to
no less a sum than 121,000,000*l*. Recalling the language,
and possibly also reviving some of the fallacies of the
mercantile system, it is apparently by some supposed
that the balance of trade, being, as it is termed, so
unfavourable to England, is an indication that at the
present time the nation is living beyond its means; that
the English people are annually spending more than they
earn, and that, in order to make good the deficit, we are
gradually using up our savings and devoting capital to
income. The maintenance of our imports at a time of
industrial depression, instead of being regarded with satisfaction, should rather, it is urged, be considered as a
measure of the prodigality with which the people are
living, and with which the nation is exhausting its resources.
Those by whom these opinions are entertained seem to
find additional cause for alarm in the fact that in hardly
any other country is there any considerable excess of imports as compared with exports, while in some countries the
exports considerably exceed the imports in value. Thus,
in the United States, this excess of exports over imports
in 1883 amounted to 20,000,000*l*., while in India it is about
21,000,000*l*. I think, however, it can be shown that the
maintenance of the present large import trade of England,
far from indicating that there is anything unsound in her
national economy, may be fairly regarded as one of the
most satisfactory features in her present condition.

In the first place, it is to be remarked, that in preparing
a statistical table of exports and imports, the value at
which any article which is imported is estimated includes
the cost of carriage, and the profits of the merchant who
imports it: whereas, in estimating the value of exports,

L

both the cost of carriage and the profits of the exporting
merchant are excluded. Thus, if a quarter of wheat is
bought at New York at 40s., and the cost of shipping this
wheat from New York to Liverpool is 4s., and the profit of
the importing merchant is 2s., its value when imported is
reckoned at 46s. In order, however, to show the different
manner in which the value of exports is estimated, let it be
assumed that a merchant buys a thousand pounds' worth of
machinery for shipment to Australia; the value of this
machinery in forming a table of exports would be stated at
1,000l. But in estimating the amount which Australia has
to transmit to England for this machinery, account has to
be taken not only of the freight, but also of the exporting
merchant's profits. Suppose that the freight is 100l., and
that the profit is 150l., Australia will pay 1,250l., and
England will receive an amount exceeding by 25 per cent.
the amount stated to be the value of the machinery exported. As by far the greater part of the foreign trade of
England is carried on in her own ships, and by her own
merchants, it follows that England receives for her exports
an amount considerably larger than is represented by the
value of these exports, because in addition to their value as
given in at the port from which they are shipped, there is to
be added the cost of carrying them to the various countries
to which they are exported, and the profits of the merchants
who export them. On the other hand, from the amount
which England has to pay for her imports, there is to be
deducted the cost of bringing them from the countries from
which they are imported. Thus, for the quarter of wheat
which is imported into Liverpool from New York, and which
is entered as worth 46s., England has to pay America only
40s.; the remaining 6s. is received by the English shipowner
and the importing merchant. England therefore has to pay
to foreign countries, for the goods she imports from them,
an amount very considerably less than is represented as the
declared value of these imports. On the other hand, she

receives from foreign countries for the goods she exports, an
amount which is much greater than that which is represented
as the declared value of these exports.   It would therefore
follow that even if the amount which she has thus to pay
for her imports were exactly equal to the amount which she
receives for her exports, there would in the Board of Trade
returns still appear to be a considerable excess in the
value of the imports when compared with the value of the
exports.   Far, however, from the existence of such an excess
being an indication that England was living beyond her
means, and was being drained of her resources, it would
simply show that our foreign trade was chiefly carried on
by our own merchants and by our own shipowners, and
that they were enjoying the profits resulting from this trade.

As previously explained, the foreign commerce of the
United States, with regard to the relative amount of imports
and exports, is in the opposite position to that of England.   The value of goods exported from the United States
considerably exceeds the value of those imported ; this is to
some extent due to the fact that a great part of the foreign
trade of the United States is carried on by English merchants
and English shipowners ; the chief portion of the profits
resulting from this trade has thus to be transmitted to England, and this makes an important addition to her aggregate
imports.   As already stated, a very large proportion, amounting (1883) to about 80 per cent., of the international commerce of the United States is carried in foreign vessels,
chiefly English.   " The international commerce of the United
States is at present mainly carried on in foreign bottoms,
which took over 70 per cent. of the aggregate imports and
exports of the fiscal year 1874-75.   Previous to the year
1860, from 75 to 80 per cent. of the total commerce was
carried on in vessels belonging to the United States."[1]   In
striking contrast with these figures, it appears that in 1877 of
the aggregate tonnage entering English ports, 70 per cent.

[1] See *Statesman's Year-Book*, 1879, p. 602.

belonged to British owners, and only 30 per cent. belonged to foreign owners.[1] When, therefore, apprehension is expressed that England is in an unsatisfactory position compared with the United States, because her imports are so largely in excess of her exports, it should be remembered that a considerable part of this excess is due to the fact that her mercantile marine is so extensive that not only the greater part of her own foreign trade, but of the foreign trade of other countries, is carried on in English ships. This, far from giving any just cause for alarm, should make us feel renewed confidence in the principles on which our present commercial system is based.

There is also another circumstance which causes the aggregate of England's imports to be considerably in excess of her exports. No other country has so large an amount of capital embarked in various foreign investments. Although it is impossible to form an exact estimate of the amount of English capital which is invested, not only in foreign loans, but also in various industrial undertakings, such as foreign mines, railways, banks, shipping companies, etc., yet it cannot be doubted that the interest which has to be annually remitted to England on the capital thus embarked represents a very considerable portion of the amount by which her imports exceed her exports. It has been calculated by competent authorities that the balance annually due to England · as interest on capital invested in India and in America alone is about 30,000,000*l*.,[2] and this debt has to be liquidated by these countries sending to England either goods or bullion. Hence the amount of the exports sent to England from America and India must not only be sufficient to pay for the goods imported from England, but must also be sufficient to pay the interest on the large amounts of English capital in-

[1] Of the total shipping of the world, the proportion of British to foreign ships in 1883 was in excess of 70 per cent., the tonnage being in round numbers 23,200,000 British, and all other countries added together 8,800,000.—M. G. F.

[2] See *Economist*, December 15, 1877.

vested in America and India. Those countries, therefore, which are largely in debt to foreign nations, must export more than they import; and in those countries which possess surplus capital and lend it abroad, the imports will exceed the exports. Consequently, the comparisons unfavourable to England which are often made by American protectionists between the industrial position of their own country and that of England, because of the large excess of English imports over exports, have so little foundation, that this excess may be regarded as affording evidence of the great extent to which they and other countries have been assisted by English capital.

Nothing can be more erroneous than to conclude that the foreign commerce of a country is in an unsatisfactory position, and that she is being drained of her resources, if it is observed that imports are largely in excess of exports, when, as in the case of England, the foreign trade is chiefly carried on by her own merchants and in her own ships, and when the amount of wealth accumulated by her people is so great that it not only suffices to supply capital for her own industry, but a large surplus annually remains to be lent to foreign governments, and to be employed in various foreign undertakings. The dread and alarm about imports exceeding exports, and about the balance of trade being unfavourable to a country, may no doubt be considered as a survival from the time when the principles of the mercantile system obtained almost universal acceptance. Thus from the remarks that are frequently made about an excess of imports, it seems to be by many supposed that when imports are in excess of exports a nation must be pursuing just the same career of extravagance as an individual who is living beyond his means, buying more than he sells, and thus steadily getting into debt. American protectionists frequently express great satisfaction because the exports from their country exceed in value the imports; they apparently consider that in this respect the industrial condition of their country compares most favourably with

that of free-trade England.   In the opinion of the French
protectionists there seems to be no weapon with which the
renewal of the Commercial Treaty with England can be so
effectually assailed, as to point out that under the operation
of that treaty the trade of France has been so entirely
changed, that whereas her exports were formerly in excess
of her imports, and she was thus enriched by foreign
commerce, now her imports exceed her exports, and she
is consequently being drained of her resources.   It can,
however, be readily shown, after the explanation which has
been given of the circumstances which cause the imports of
a country to exceed the exports, that the present position
of the foreign commerce of the United States, far from
affording any justification for a protectionist policy, may be
regarded as greatly strengthening the case in favour of free
trade.   If the goods which America sends to England
exceed in value those which she receives from England,
it is evident that America is in debt to England; and that
this indebtedness is due to the fact that she has borrowed
capital from England, and that, in carrying on her foreign
trade, she is largely employing English ships and English
merchants.   Such indebtedness cannot be an advantage,
but must be a disadvantage to a country, and therefore, so
far as it is due to protection, it may be considered as
evidence of the injury inflicted on America by a policy
of commercial restriction.   There is also no circumstance
connected with the present commercial position of the
United States which should be regarded by the people of
that country with more apprehension than the decline in
her shipping trade which is shown by the large extent to
which her foreign commerce is carried on in English ships
and by English merchants.   The protective duties which
are imposed by the tariff of the United States on iron,
copper, wood and almost all the other materials which are
employed in shipbuilding add so much to the cost of
constructing a ship, that the shipping interest in the United

States has declined to a most serious extent with the increase in recent years of her protective duties. It has already been stated that 80 per cent. of the entire commerce of the United States is now carried on in foreign bottoms; whereas previous to 1860 between 75 and 80 per cent. of that commerce was carried ·in her own ships. Again, with regard to the change which has lately taken place in the foreign commerce of France, it appears that whereas the French people used to send abroad more than was received back in return, they now receive more than they send to foreign countries: in other words, while France used to be in debt to foreign countries, foreign countries are now in debt to her. So far as this alteration in her position is due to her Commercial Treaty with England it will be scarcely denied that the existence of that Treaty ought to be a subject for congratulation rather than regret.

The statistics of the English exports and imports of bullion and specie during the last few years show in a very striking manner that a great excess of imports over exports may be entirely due to the circumstances before explained. Instead of there being any drain of money from England to adjust a so-called unfavourable balance of trade, the amount of bullion and specie which has been imported into England during the fifteen years from 1869 to 1883 has exceeded by no less than 37,000,000*l.* the amount which has been exported; although during this period the aggregate value of her imports exceeded by no less than 1,380,000,000*l.* the value of her exports. It therefore appears that so large an excess of imports over exports, as that which characterises the foreign trade of England, need not necessarily be accompanied by any drain of bullion or of specie; for during the period when this excess of imports has been most marked, England has on the average of years been adding about 2,500,000*l.* to her stock of bullion and specie, and this is supposed to be the amount which is annually required for fresh coinage and for various manufacturing purposes.[1]

In attempting to draw a favourable instead of an unfavourable conclusion as to the commercial position of England, from the fact that while there has been a considerable decline in her export trade, her imports have rather increased than diminished, nothing is farther from my intention than to deny that there has been very severe depression in many important branches of industry. As this industrial depression is not unfrequently attributed to the policy of free trade which has been adopted by England, it is important to prove that, far from protection being an antidote to industrial depression, protectionist countries such as the United States were not during the depression in a more satisfactory position than England. It sometimes however seems to be supposed that much darker days are in store for England, and that she has hitherto been able to ward off the worst consequences of bad trade by a series of artificial expedients, which can be only looked upon as temporary shifts. How, it is asked, can a nation, without burdening herself with debt, and laying up for herself a store of future embarrassment, continue to spend as much at a time when trade was bad, as when it was in a state of exceptional prosperity. During the depression the amount of goods imported into England showed no falling off; the people continued to purchase, even more largely than they did before, all the foreign products which minister either to their wants or to their enjoyments. It is generally admitted that the quantity of tea which is annually consumed by the English people affords a very correct index of the prosperity of the country. When there is a bad harvest at home there is naturally a large increase in the importation of wheat. When however it is found that there is a great addition to the quantity of tea which is imported and retained for home consumption, the conclusion is irresistible that the people can

[1] See *Statistical Abstract*, 1884.

afford to spend a larger sum on an article which may be regarded to some extent as a luxury. The quantity of tea, which has been imported into England and retained for home consumption, has increased in a very striking manner since 1862. In that year the quantity so imported was 78,793,977 lbs.; in 1877, a year that is constantly spoken of as one of exceptional depression, the quantity was 151,114,886 lbs., or an increase of nearly 100 per cent.; and in 1883 the amount was 170,780,777 lbs. A part of the increase between 1862 and 1877 may no doubt be attributed to the fact that the duty on tea had been reduced between those years from 1s. 5d. to 6d. a lb. It is however worthy of special remark, as bearing on the subject we are now considering, that the consumption of tea during the period of commercial depression continued steadily to increase, and that this consumption was much larger than it was when the trade of the country was in a state of the greatest activity. The years 1872–3–4 are frequently referred to as a time when English trade was at the zenith of its prosperity. The quantity of tea imported and retained for home consumption in these three years respectively was :—

1872.	1873.	1874.
127,661,360 lbs.	131,881,476 lbs.	137,279,891 lbs.

The industrial depression is generally thought to have commenced in the closing months of 1874, and for some years it increased in intensity. Yet in these years, the annual increase in the consumption of tea was fully maintained; the quantity retained for home consumption being :—

1876.	1878.	1880.	1882.
149,104,194 lbs.	157,396,661 lbs.	158,321,572 lbs.	164,958,230 lbs.
1877.	1879.	1881.	1883.
151,114,886 lbs.	160,432,284 lbs.	160,051,314 lbs.	170,780,777 lbs.

No part of the increased consumption of tea which took

place in these later years was due to a reduction of duty, for the duty has remained unchanged since 1866.

It may be thought that such a state of things as that just described cannot continue, and that if in a period of industrial depression a nation purchases more largely articles of general consumption, savings are either being used up or future liabilities are being incurred. The benefit which is conferred on a nation as a whole in a period of such exceptional industrial activity as that of a few years since, is, I believe, by no means so great or so widely diffused as is commonly supposed. It can, I think, be shown that such prosperity is accompanied by some very serious drawbacks ; that the advantages which result from it are by no means diffused over the entire nation ; and that although at such a time many are enriched, yet the additional wealth which they secure cannot be regarded as so much pure gain ; a portion of it at least represents a forced contribution from some of their less fortunate fellow-countrymen.

Those who suppose that great industrial activity necessarily implies an increase of well-being to the entire community, may be asked to consider what was the effect on the nation generally of the extraordinary prosperity which was some years since enjoyed by the coal and iron trades. A sudden increase in the demand for coal, consequent to a large extent on an increased demand for iron, produced an unprecedented rise in the price of coal, the rise being no less than 13s. 6d. a ton. It has been frequently asserted that this rise was chiefly brought about by the action of trades-unionists, who, taking advantage of the increased demand for labour at a time when trade was exceptionally active, forced up wages to such a point that their employers were obliged to advance the price of coal in order to compensate themselves for the higher wages which they were compelled to pay. It has, however, been conclusively established that so small a portion of the increase in the price of coal was due to the cause just mentioned, that a

rise of 2s. 6d. a ton would have been amply sufficient to
compensate the employer for the extra wages which he paid.¹
By far the greater part of the increased value which coal
suddenly acquired must therefore be regarded as affording a
source from which an enormous addition was made to the
income obtained by the fortunate owners or lessees of coal
mines. On every ton of coal raised there was at least an
additional 11s. to be given either to the owner or to the
lessee of the mine. Profits in this industry consequently
advanced with unprecedented rapidity. The annual output
of coal at the time was about 120,000,000 tons. Consequently the rise in the price of coal caused no less a sum
than 66,000,000l. in a single year to be distributed among
the owners and lessees of mines, whereas the amount distributed in the form of extra wages was not more than
15,000,000l. As the aggregate production and consumption
of English coal was at the time about 120,000,000 tons, it
follows that the rise in price of 13s. 6d. a ton caused no less
a sum than 81,000,000l. sterling to be taken in a single
year from the consumers of this coal. As the export
of coal from England at that time was not more than
12,000,000 tons, nine-tenths of this enormous sum, or
about 72,000,000l., had in this single year to be contributed by the consumers of coal in England. A portion
of this amount was no doubt repaid to England by foreign

¹ See Report of the Select Committee of the House of Commons
appointed in 1873 to inquire into the causes which had produced the
recent rise in the price of coal. From some evidence given before this
Committee it appears that the rise in the price of coal was greater and the
advance in the wages of the workmen less than above estimated. Thus,
in a table given in the Evidence at page 191, it is stated that in the
West Yorkshire district, between October 1871 and March 1873, there
was an advance in the price of coal at the pit's mouth of 15s. 5d. a ton,
while wages at this period were advanced only 1s. 1½d. a ton. During
this time the price of coal was raised on eight different occasions, while
on only five occasions was there any rise in wages. In every single
instance the rise in wages was subsequent to the rise in the price of coal.

countries. A rise in the price of coal increases the cost of all those articles in the manufacture of which coal is used. The price of such articles will consequently have to be advanced in order to compensate those who produce them. When therefore an article, the price of which is thus advanced, is exported, the burden of the extra price falls, not upon the English producer or merchant, but upon the foreign consumer. A part therefore of the loss which was caused to the consumers of English coal, no doubt fell, not only upon those foreign countries which used English coal, but also upon the foreign consumers of various English products. When, however, the most ample allowance has been made for this circumstance, the fact still remains that so great a rise in the price of coal must have inflicted a most serious loss on the general body of the English people; the nature and extent of this loss have, I believe, not yet received adequate consideration.

Unprecedented as were the gains of the owners and lessees of coal mines, and important as was the addition made to the wages of those who were employed in these mines, yet it should not be forgotten that the advantage thus secured was to a great extent purchased at the expense of the general community. A rise in the price of coal must be just as severely felt by the people as if a first necessary of life were subjected to a heavy tax. It is an impost from which the humblest cannot escape. An income-tax may be so adjusted that the poor do not contribute to it, but in such a climate as that of England fuel is scarcely less essential than food; and no small portion of the enormous fortunes which were realised when the coal famine was at its height may be regarded as made up from the forced contributions of the very poorest in the land. The annual consumption of coal for household purposes, in England, is estimated at 20,000,000 tons. Consequently when coal rises 13s. 6d. a ton the English people have annually to pay 13,500,000l. more for the coal which is used for household purposes. An extra tax is thus imposed upon them not less in amount than half the interest on the National Debt. Such a tax, onerous though it is, represents only a portion of the heavy impost which is levied by a rise in the price of coal. Such a rise must directly lead to the price of all those articles being advanced, in the manufacture of which coal is employed. It has been calculated that it requires about $2\frac{1}{2}$ tons of coal to smelt one ton of iron; consequently if the cost of the coal with which a ton of iron is smelted is increased by 1*l.* 13*s.* 9*d.* there must be a corresponding addition to the price of iron. Every one therefore who wants to purchase any article of hardware will have to pay considerably more for it. Manufacturers and farmers will find machinery and implements materially increased in price; every steam-engine will also have to be worked at a much greater cost; and in order that the manufacturers may be compensated for these increased charges it will be necessary that the price of the articles which they produce shall be advanced. One result of the recent industrial inactivity has been that the price of coal has been reduced to its former level; the country has consequently been relieved of a most serious burden. The advantage which has thus been gained by the general body of the people ought to be regarded as a not inconsiderable compensation for the losses which have undoubtedly been brought on certain special classes by depression of trade. It is well that the subject should be looked at from this point of view, in order that the fears of those may be allayed, who appear to be alarmed because the industrial depression from which the country has suffered has not been more widespread in its effects, and has not exerted a more marked influence on the general condition of the country.

During the continuance of this depression, not only was there no falling off in the demand for articles of general consumption, but there were other and more positive indications that the industrial depression, severely as it affected certain trades and certain localities, did not produce so great an effect upon the general condition of the country as was usually supposed. If the amount of pauperism during the four years 1871–74, a period of exceptional industrial activity, is compared with the amount in the four years 1875–78, which mark the period of extreme depression, it appears that there was in these last four years a very remarkable diminution in pauperism. This is shown by the following table, which gives the number of persons, exclusive of vagrants, who were in receipt of parochial relief in England and Wales on the 1st of January, in each year :—

1871	1,081,926
1872	977,664
1873	890,372
1874	829,281
1875	815,587
1876	749,593
1877	728,350
1878	742,703 [1]

There was also a similar decline during the same years in the pauperism of Scotland and Ireland.

The striking diminution of pauperism which is shown by the above figures, was no doubt partly due to an improved administration of the poor-law. Within the last few years there has been an increasing tendency to restrict out-door relief; and the decline in pauperism has taken place almost entirely through a reduction in the number of out-door paupers. But making the fullest allowance for this circum-

[1] There was a slight increase in 1879 and 1880, but since 1880 there has again been a considerable decline in pauperism in England, Wales and Scotland. The economic and political circumstances of Ireland during the same period were exceptionally unfortunate, and here alone the increase in pauperism which marked the years 1879 and 1880 has been maintained. The total number of paupers in 1884 was in England and Wales 774,310, considerably less therefore than in the years of the greatest commercial prosperity.—M. G. F.

stance it is still very significant that during a period of great industrial depression, there was an almost continuous decline in pauperism.

Other facts may be adduced which clearly indicate that the industrial depression, from which the trade of England has suffered, although most severely felt in certain localities, did not produce so great an effect as is commonly supposed upon the general condition of the country. In a period of wide-spread national distress there would inevitably be a marked diminution in the amount of Savings Banks deposits, accompanied by a considerable increase in the sums withdrawn. Taking 1873 as a year of maximum trade activity, and comparing it with 1877, a year of severe depression, it is found that in 1877 the amount deposited in the Savings Banks was 19,373,009*l.*, and this amount exceeds by no less a sum than 2,151,033*l.* the amount deposited in 1873.[1] The amount withdrawn in 1877 exceeded the amount withdrawn in 1873 by a sum almost exactly equivalent to the increase in the amount deposited. The considerable increase in the withdrawals from Savings Banks undoubtedly shows that there was severe distress in certain localities; but the counterbalancing increase in the deposits proves that the capacity to save of the general body of the people was not affected, and that the loss suffered by the working classes in certain localities was accompanied by an improvement in their condition in other localities.

The traffic returns of the railways may be referred to as affording another proof that the inactivity in some special branches of trade produced much less effect on the general condition of the country than is usually supposed. From the complaints constantly made about the stagnation of

[1] These figures are arrived at by adding together the sums deposited at the Post Office Savings Bank and the Trustee Saving Banks. The amount thus deposited in 1883 was 24,123,196*l.*, or nearly seven millions more than in 1873.—M. G. F.

business it might be fairly concluded that there would have been a serious falling off in the traffic returns of the railways. There was, however, no such falling off. On the contrary, again comparing the years 1873 and 1877, it will be found that in the latter year the number of miles of railway open in the United Kingdom had increased, and that the gross receipts per mile had also increased from 4,139*l.* in 1873 to 4,198*l.* in 1877.[1]

The facts which have just been quoted have not been brought forward with the intention of showing that depressed trade is no disadvantage to a country: the object I have had in view, is to point out that an exaggerated estimate is habitually made of the benefit which the nation derives from special branches of industry enjoying exceptional prosperity. A large portion of the additional wealth which appears to be created when certain trades are unusually active, really represents no increase whatever in the aggregate wealth of the nation. It is simply a transfer of wealth from the general public to a special class: the few are enriched by the contributions of the many. When, for instance, it was said that the coal trade was in a deplorable condition, it would be altogether erroneous to conclude that the production of coal had greatly diminished, and that less coal was used than formerly. On the contrary, the production of coal increased. In 1873, the year of maximum prices, 127,016,747 tons of coal were produced; in 1877, a year of extreme depression, 134,610,763 tons of coal were produced.[2] Within these

---

[1] If these figures are brought up to the present time it is seen that 1883 fully maintains the advance noted in 1877. Whereas in 1877 the number of miles of railway open was 12,098, in 1883 it was 13,202; the number of passengers carried in the year had risen during the same time from 490,351,707, to 612,401,758; the tons of goods and minerals conveyed had advanced from 178,872,570 to 225,909,383, and the gross receipts per mile from 4198*l.* to 4417*l.*—M. G. F.

[2] In 1882, the latest date for which the information is available, the tons of coal raised had advanced to 156,499,977.—M. G. F.

four years there had been no doubt a great decline in the
profits of the coal-owners, and a very considerable falling
off in the wages of the colliers ; but, on the other hand, the
consumers of coal, representing the entire nation, enjoyed
the great advantage of having to pay 13s. or 14s. less for
every ton of coal they purchased. The community was in-
fact relieved of a most onerous burden of many millions a
year. Although, therefore, the coal-owners and those whom
they employ were much less well-off than they were before,
and had consequently to reduce their expenditure, yet as
what was lost by them was to a great extent gained by the
rest of the nation, there is no reason why the amount which
the nation can expend on articles of general consumption
should diminish. This no doubt indicates one reason why,
as previously shown, the consumption of articles in general
use has not decreased ; and why, throughout the continuance of the depression, the import trade of the country
was so well maintained.

The remarks which have been made in reference to the
coal trade apply to many other industries. The fall in
prices has widely extended, and in every instance in which
it has occurred it is equally true, as pointed out in regard
to the price of coal, that a considerable portion of that
which is lost by the producer is gained by the consumer.
It is no doubt a serious disadvantage to mill-owners and
operatives that cotton and woollen goods should not sell
for as much as before ; but, at the same time, the fact
should not be lost sight of, that it is a great advantage
to all the people who wish to purchase these goods, that
they are able to buy them more cheaply than formerly.
In discussions with regard to the effect on the country of a
particular state of trade, attention is generally entirely concentrated on the interest of the producer ; and the interest
of the consumer is passed over almost unnoticed. The inflation of prices which occurs in a period of great activity
inflicts a severe injury upon all that numerous class whose

incomes are fixed in pecuniary amount. The annuitant, the fundholder, the person in receipt of a fixed salary, the numerous class whose wages do not vary with the state of trade, all these suffer severely when prices are forced up in a period of exceptionally active trade; their income or their earnings remaining the same, while almost everything they have to purchase is becoming dearer, they do not receive any compensation for the loss which is thus inflicted upon them. As they find that their incomes possess less and less purchasing power, it is no advantage for them to hear that certain persons, possibly the fortunate owners of a mineral monopoly, are becoming rich with unprecedented rapidity.

If a comparison is made between the prices of articles of general consumption in England in 1873 and 1878, it will be at once seen that there was a fall sufficient to produce a not inconsiderable reduction in the cost of living.[1] It has been estimated that this fall in prices reduced the cost of maintaining the household of an artisan on the average from 7 to 8 per cent. in the period referred to.[2] It therefore appears that all those who are in the receipt of fixed pecuniary incomes, whether these incomes are derived from investments, salaries or wages, are decidedly better off than they were when the trade of the country was in a state of maximum activity, and when the nation was said to be enjoying unusual prosperity. The persons, who are in the position just described, constitute a numerous and important section of the community, and the addition which has thus been virtually made to their incomes enables them to become larger purchasers of articles of general consumption. An extra demand for these articles is thus created, which may counterbalance the falling-off in the demand of those who are employed in the trades which have been specially depressed, and whose wages have consequently been con-

---

[1] A comparison of prices between 1878 and 1884 shows that the reduction in the cost of living is maintained.—M. G. F.

[2] See *Economist*, 20th April, 1878.

siderably reduced.   It is also to be borne in mind, that
this fall in the prices of articles of general consumption
makes a reduction in wages less serious than it otherwise
would be.

It would be scarcely appropriate, in discussing the subject
of protection and free trade, to attempt to investigate all the
economic phenomena associated with a period of commercial depression.   I have, however, thought it desirable to
consider those aspects of the subject to which attention has
been here directed, because it is important to show whether,
in periods of industrial depression, the effects which are produced by such depression are more serious to a country
which has adopted a policy of free trade, than they are to
a country which maintains a system of protection.   In view
of the disappointment which is sometimes expressed, that
after England has so long adopted free trade, severe depression should have fallen on some branches of her industry, it becomes important to show that although the
effects of this depression have been more severely felt in
protectionist than in free-trade countries, yet if the commerce of every country were as entirely freed from protective
restrictions, as is the commerce of England, periods of depressed trade would inevitably occur.   The depression from
which various branches of industry have lately been suffer·
ing, may be regarded as the natural outcome of the prosperity which these same industries were enjoying a few
years since.   It is hardly more certain that night will follow
day, or that winter will follow summer, than that a period of
exceptional prosperity in trade will be succeeded by a period
of corresponding depression.   The extremely high profits
which were realised by coal-owners and iron-masters in the
years 1871–74 undoubtedly produced the low rate of profit
returned to capital invested in these industries during the
period of depression which subsequently ensued.   Whenever any particular trade becomes exceptionally remunerative, people eagerly strive to share the advantages which

that trade offers; a largely increased amount of capital is pressed into it; new mines are opened, or new works or manufactories are built, and the means of production are greatly extended. If, as almost invariably happens, the causes which in the first instance produced the exceptional activity do not permanently continue, the demand is not maintained, and those engaged in the trade are in the position of possessing appliances for a great increase in the supply, at a time when there is either a diminution of the demand, or when there is no increase corresponding to the larger supply. The inevitable consequence is a rapid fall in prices, and a diminution in profits and wages, such as that which has taken place in all those industries which were most prosperous a few years since.

It has already been shown that when the coal trade was most depressed, the quantity of coal raised, and also the quantity used in England, were greater than they were five years previously, when the price of coal was exceptionally high. The high prices which then prevailed, and the large profits which were then realised, caused many new mines to be opened, and the works in existing mines to be greatly extended. This particular branch of industry being thus much enlarged, an increased quantity of coal has been annually raised; but as the circumstances which caused an exceptionally active demand for coal in 1873 ceased to operate, the additional coal raised could not be sold except at a considerable reduction in price. Unless an industry becomes depressed in consequence of a permanent falling off in the demand, or in consequence of the demand being satisfied from some cheaper source, it is perfectly certain that the depression cannot permanently continue. When profits are exceptionally low, there is just the same inducement to contract a business as there is to extend it when profits are exceptionally high; the supply will thus become restricted, there will be a tendency for prices to rise, and a sudden increase in the demand may again produce an unusual rise in.

prices, and thus exceptional prosperity and exceptional depression succeed each other in regular cycles. As an example, it
may be mentioned that within the last fifty years there have
been in the English cotton trade five periods of great prosperity, succeeded in each instance by periods of corresponding depression. The large returns which are yielded both
to capital and labour in periods of prosperity should be
regarded as exceptional. The employers and the employed
in any trade should never fail to remember that the equalising force of competition is ever present to prevent an
abnormally high rate of profit and wages being permanently secured by those engaged in any particular branch
of industry. Consequently a portion of the remuneration
which is secured both by capital and labour in a time of
exceptional activity, should be regarded as a reserve, to
compensate the employers and the employed for the
reduction in profits and wages which will inevitably ensue.

As an opinion seems prevalent that all fluctuations in the
prosperity of English industry are due to free trade, I have
thought it desirable to show in some detail that the recent
depression was in many instances to be regarded as a
natural rebound from the previous exceptional activity. It
is however important to bear in mind that depression may
be produced by many other causes—causes moreover quite
as independent of free trade as the one to which reference
has just been made. Thus it has not unfrequently happened that a change in taste or fashion has most seriously
diminished the demand for a particular article. If the
change should continue, the falling off in the demand may
be permanent, and the trade will gradually decline. The
invention of some new machine, although it may powerfully promote the development of a trade, yet may most
prejudicially affect some special branch of industry which
is supplanted by the new machine. It is well known how
long and hopeless was the struggle which was carried on
against machinery by the handloom weavers, and many

in our own time have witnessed a similar struggle on the part of the Spitalfields silk-weavers. The distress of these weavers and the decline of their industry have been often referred to by those who are opposed to free trade. It can however be shown that this decline commenced before free trade was introduced, and when the English silk trade was protected against foreign competition by the imposition of an import duty of 30 per cent. on foreign silks. In 1837, Dr. James P. Kay (afterwards better known as Sir James Kay-Shuttleworth) was appointed by the Poor Law Board to inquire into the great distress prevailing among the Spitalfields weavers, and as to the necessity for, and the best means of relief. From Dr. Kay's report it appears that out of 14,000 looms one-third were altogether disused, and that certain of the remaining looms were only partially employed. The chief manufacturers, he stated, were of opinion that the wages of the weaving population had fallen from 10,000*l.* to 12,000*l.*, to 5,000*l.* to 6,000*l.* per week, and the distress was so great that appeals for assistance were repeatedly made to the Government and to private individuals. In a period of six or eight months, from 1825-26, the sum so received exceeded 30,000*l.*[1]

When considering the causes which produce industrial depression, it is for many reasons desirable to make special reference to the effect which may be exercised on agriculture by unpropitious seasons. Although there may be differences of opinion as to the extent to which the depression now prevailing in English agriculture is to be attributed to unfavourable seasons, yet no one can deny that the repeated unfavourable seasons between 1875 and 1883 have exercised a very powerful effect in bringing about this

[1] My attention was first called to this interesting report by Mr. Thomas G. Atkins, of 9, Blossom Street, Norton Folgate, from whom I have received many able letters, not only on protection, but on other economic questions, such as poor law administration. Mr. Atkins was working as a Spitalfields weaver at the time referred to in Dr. Kay's report.

depression. Although it may now be impossible to foresee the future effect which may be exercised on the prices of agricultural products by increased importations from America and other countries, yet it is clear that these importations have enabled the country to get through eight bad or indifferent harvests in succession, not only without severe distress, but with a simultaneous diminution in pauperism, an increase in the consumption of the necessaries of life, and an augmentation in the Savings Bank deposits. If there had been the same number of unpropitious seasons between 1830 and 1840 as there have been during the last ten years, the Corn Laws and the protective duties which were then in operation would have no doubt caused a great advance in prices. In all probability prices would have attained almost a famine point, and an incalculable amount of suffering would have been caused to the entire community. The comparative comfort which has been enjoyed by all classes, even including the agricultural labourers, during the present period of agricultural depression, shows with striking distinctness that although unpropitious seasons cause severe losses to the capital invested in agriculture, yet the suffering to the rest of the community is restricted within the narrowest possible limits when the deficiencies in our own crops can be supplied by free importations from other countries.

It cannot be too carefully borne in mind that the cultivator, as distinguished from the owner of the land, has no direct interest in the maintenance of a high level of prices. High or low prices is merely a question of high or low rents.[1]

---

[1] Mr. James Howard, M.P., a well-known authority on agricultural matters, in a paper read at the Farmers' Club, December 8th, 1884, supports the view expressed above that the chief remedy for agricultural distress, in so far as it has been brought about by low prices, is a corresponding reduction in rents. He points out that much of the prevailing distress is due to the mischief done while the corn laws were in operation, in causing poor clay lands which were then pasture to be broken up and converted into arable land. Farms mainly composed of such land now yield no rent, but if they had been left in pasture, they would

As already shown, the effect which the Corn Laws would exert in the average of years in raising prices was over estimated. Rents were consequently calculated on the supposition that prices would be higher than they actually were, and the farmers consequently suffered severe losses. If it should be subsequently found that in consequence of an increase of foreign importations, or from any other cause, such as an appreciation in the value of gold, a low level of agricultural prices should permanently prevail, a re-adjustment of rents would then of course become necessary. For many years after the introduction of free trade the rapid increase in wealth produced so great an augmentation in the demand for food, that prices advanced in spite of additional importations. The statistics which have been quoted on the authority of Mr. Caird show that between 1857 and 1875 there was a marked and steady increase in rents. Farms were at that time so actively competed for that for every farm to let there were at least twenty or thirty applicants. So great was the anxiety to obtain farms, that in numerous instances farmers rented far more land than they had capital properly to culti-vate. Advances were freely made to them by bankers and others; these advances have now to be repaid under the most adverse circumstances, and the extent to which farming was carried on upon credit has of course most

pay a good rent. With regard to the efficacy of an import duty on wheat as a remedy for agricultural depression, Mr. Howard points out "that neither in Scotland nor Ireland is wheat more than a mere fraction of the cereal crops; the proportion in Scotland indeed is only 5 per cent. of the cultivated area, and in Ireland only 4 per cent.; whereas in England it is 38 per cent. Is it to be supposed for a moment that if the staple crop of the English farmer is to be protected by an import duty, the Scotchman with his 76 per cent. or the Irishman with his 84 per cent. of oats, will be content that his produce shall be exposed to the rigours of free trade, whilst at the same time he is compelled him-self to pay an increased price for all the wheat and flour he is obliged to buy?" (Farm Rents present, past, and future, by James Howard, M. P.) —M. G. F.

seriously added to the difficulties of the present period of depression.

In making these remarks on agricultural depression I do not intend to ignore the effect which may possibly be produced by increased importations of agricultural products from America and other countries. It may, of course, happen that the continuance of low prices may necessitate a permanent reduction of rents, and may produce a fall in the value of agricultural land in England. It also seems inevitable that one consequence of the increase in importations will be to bring about a very important change in the system of English agriculture. Such a product as wheat, which can not only be cheaply grown abroad, but can be cheaply imported, may not improbably be grown to a smaller extent in England, and our soil will be more largely used for the raising of such products as milk, vegetables, and meat, which can only be imported under greater difficulties and at greater cost. At the present time the fall in the value of wheat land is so much greater than the fall in the value of pasture land, that a not inconsiderable area of arable land is being converted into permanent pasture. This conversion, which will involve a considerable outlay, affords a striking example of the mischief which is done by attempting to give an artificial assistance to industry. Much of the land, which is now being laid down to permanent grass, was originally meadow or downland. This was broken up with the object of growing corn when corn was made artificially dear by protective duties. Not only will great expense be required to restore the land to grass, but in many cases it will never again become as good for purposes of pasture as it was originally. For instance, on Salisbury Plain there are thousands of acres of down-land that have been broken up, which will now hardly pay to be cultivated. It seems impossible to bring it back to the same state as it was in before it was broken up; weeds take the place of a sweet and short herbage, and yet this land, if it were now in down, would be of the greatest use in the breeding of sheep, which is at present the most profitable branch of English agriculture.

Enough has probably been said to show that any resort to protection by the imposition of import duties on food would supply no remedy for agricultural depression. The utmost it would do would be to give some temporary relief to farmers at the cost of an incalculable amount of mischief to the rest of the country. Any advantage which the farmers might receive from an increase of prices would be ultimately appropriated not by them but by the owners of land in the form of increased rents. With regard to the depression that until recently affected many other branches of industry besides agriculture, any departure from a policy of free trade would not only have delayed the revival of commercial prosperity, but would have greatly aggravated the effect of this depression whilst it continued. It has been shown from the statistics of pauperism, and other facts which have been adduced, that this depression exerted very much less effect on the general condition of the country than is usually supposed. No circumstance has probably so much contributed to enable the country thus to tide over a period of bad trade as the reduction in the cost of living, which has resulted from the fall in the price of many articles of general consumption. When an article of general consumption is cheapened, the loss to the producer may be compensated by a gain to the consumer. Under a system of protection, however, there is no chance of bringing into operation such an influence to neutralise the consequences of depressed trade. An exactly opposite course is pursued, for by increasing the price of various commodities, through the imposition of protective duties, the cost of living is increased, and the general consumer is taxed in order to benefit the producer. In the United States, import duties are imposed on no less than 1,500 different articles. In England every article that is imported, except seven or eight, is admitted to her ports duty free. This increase in the cost of living so much aggravated the effects of depressed trade, that a few years since, in 1877-78, when the depression was at its height, workmen left the United States in large numbers in order to return to England. From all the facts which can be most relied upon as showing the general condition of a country, it may be concluded that the industrial depression was more severely felt in the United States than in England. Throughout the continuance of this depression there has been an almost continuous decline of pauperism in England. Her people purchased an increased quantity of articles of general consumption ; the traffic returns of her railways were augmented ; and the amount deposited in the Savings Banks increased. In the United States, on the contrary, there was, during the same period, a steady increase in pauperism and destitution. Thus, in the State of Massachusetts, the number of vagrants so largely increased, that whereas 43,000 were relieved in 1873, the number in 1876 was not less than 148,000. Whilst the traffic returns of the English railways were maintained, the American railways had to bear such disastrous losses, that in 1876 and 1877 no fewer than eighty-four railways, covering 7,721 miles, were sold under foreclosure.[1] Industrial depression produced such widespread distress in the United States, that labour disputes induced the workmen to make socialistic demands, such as, for many years, have scarcely been heard of in England. The people of America, having been long accustomed by the system of protection to look to the State for aid in their industry, not unnaturally seek State assistance in a time of trade depression ; and demands which may assume a serious communistic development were made by unemployed American workmen, that the municipal authorities should find work for all applicants.

[1] See Paper read by the Right Honourable A. J. Mundella, M.P., before the Statistical Society of London on February 19th, 1878.

In a petition which was in 1878 presented by some of the leading merchants and manufacturers in the United States to the Senate and House of Representatives, in favour of unrestricted trade, it is stated that there was at the time "unspeakable distress" among the working classes in America. It is also said, "Pauperism and crime increase daily within our borders; skilled mechanics tramp the country over in vain search for the means of living; and instances are not lacking where some of our best artisans have been induced to leave our shores to accept the so-called 'pauper wages' of other countries. . . . A day's labour in England will purchase from twenty-five to thirty per cent. more than a day's labour in the United States." From this and other similar evidence which might be adduced it is evident that the maintenance of a system of protection to a great extent neutralises the advantage of the unequalled natural resources of the United States, and indefinitely increases the difficulties which have to be encountered in those periods of depression which are certain to recur.

In attempting to show the effects produced on a free trade, and a protectionist country, respectively, in a time of industrial depression, a comparison might be made, not simply between England and the United States, but between England, Germany, Russia and other countries, where a policy of commercial restriction is still maintained. I have, however, been induced to contrast the condition of England and the United States, because in Russia and Germany, for instance, other circumstances are in operation which are independent of tariffs, and which materially affect the industrial condition of those countries. Russia had recently to bear the strain of a costly war; and there can be no doubt that the military system which is maintained in Germany, and in other Continental countries, exerts a most important influence on their industrial economy. Not only are the resources of these countries severely taxed by

their enormous armies, but even a more serious loss is inflicted on them by the conscription, which draws away from
industrial pursuits a large proportion of their population
at the very period of life when they could render to the
nation the most valuable services as productive labourers.
Men have to devote themselves to military training, and to
learning military manœuvres, at the time when they are
best fitted to acquire skill in some handicraft. It is scarcely
possible to over-estimate the direct and indirect loss which
is thus inflicted on a community. Taking the last figures
accessible,[1] it appears that the following is the strength, on
a peace footing, of the armies of the five chief European
Powers :—

Germany	449,000
Austria	290,000
Russia	770,000
France	491,000
Italy	714,000
TOTAL	2,714,000

These five Powers consequently have to bear, even in a
time of peace, the enormous burden of maintaining more
than 2,700,000 men in arms. Not only has the direct cost
of their maintenance to be borne, but this vast number of
men, in the prime of life, are drawn away from industrial
pursuits. In order, however, to form an adequate idea of
the loss caused to these countries by this rivalry in military
armaments, which was inaugurated with the advent of the
Second Empire in France, it is necessary to bear in mind
that so large a proportion of the entire population have to
spend some of the best years of life in military training,
that these armies, immense though they are in time of peace,
can be immediately trebled or quadrupled if it is decided
to place them on a war footing. In face of such facts as
these, I feel that it would be unfair to make a comparison

[1] See *Statesman's Year-Book*, 1884.

between the industrial condition of Germany and England, and attribute the greater severity with which the industrial depression was felt in the former country to the policy of protection which she so zealously maintains.   It could be easily shown that the depression in her trade, and the widespread distress which prevailed amongst her workmen, were most materially aggravated, as was the case in the United States, by the system of commercial restriction which she so tenaciously supports ; but it cannot be denied that this depression and this distress were largely due to the perpetual incubus imposed upon industrial development by such a military system as that which is maintained in Germany and other Continental countries.

CHAPTER VI.

In considering the subject of commercial treaties, I think it at once becomes evident that the desirability of entering in any particular case into such a treaty does not simply depend on economic considerations. It is perfectly possible that a commercial treaty, by increasing the friendly intercourse between two countries, may produce social and political advantages which would provide an ample compensation for any disadvantage involved in the departure from sound economic principles. It would be beyond the scope of this book to attempt to estimate the social and political consequences of a commercial treaty. Although, however, I think a serious mistake would be committed if the negotiation of a commercial treaty in any particular instance should be decided solely on economic grounds, yet it is desirable that these economic consequences should be carefully considered.

It has been maintained by many high authorities that it is impossible for a country like England, which has adopted a policy of complete free trade, to negotiate a commercial treaty without departing in some degree from strict principle and from logical consistency. This opinion, which was frequently expressed during the Corn Law debates, was revived during the discussions on the Commercial Treaty with France in 1860. It was then supported with great ability by Lord Overstone, and more recently arguments in favour of this view of the case have been most ably urged by Lord Grey,[1] who, like Lord Overstone, has throughout a long life been a staunch supporter of the principles of free trade. It is thought by those who hold these opinions that the negotiation of a commercial treaty involves some sacrifice of principle; because, in accordance with the doctrines of free trade, import duties are imposed solely for purposes of revenue, and those particular duties are levied which it is supposed can be raised with the least inconvenience. Thus a large proportion of the tobacco which is consumed in England is imported from America. England levies a very heavy duty upon tobacco, because it is thought to be a convenient and desirable mode of obtaining revenue, and not with the object of retaliating upon America for the many protective import duties which she imposes upon English goods. If from any circumstance the importation of tobacco from America should cease—if, for example, all tobacco was obtained from countries whose tariffs were much more liberal towards England than that of the United States, this would not affect the continuance of the tobacco duty in England; for the duty is maintained because it is considered to be a desirable mode of obtaining a portion of the revenue which is required, and neither the amount of revenue needed, nor the comparative advantages of some particular form of taxation, would in the slightest degree be affected by a change in the locality from which the imported article is procured. As it thus appears that the amount and character of the import duties which are maintained by a free-trade country are determined solely by considerations of revenue, it is urged that if the lowering or raising of these duties is made to depend upon the tariff changes that may be introduced by other countries, a certain sanction is at once given to a policy of reciprocity. As an example, it has been said that if in our negotiations for a commercial

---

[1] See the *Times*, August 27th and September 2nd, 1881.

treaty with France it should be stipulated that the duties on
wine imported into England should be reduced if certain
reductions were made in the French tariff, then one of the
two following alternatives might occur:—If the reduction
in the wine duties was desirable, we might, in the event of
France refusing to alter her tariff, preclude ourselves from
carrying out a beneficial change in our fiscal system; if, on
the other hand, the reduction of the wine duties was not
desirable in itself, we should to a certain extent be sacri-
ficing our own system of taxation in order to secure certain
improvements in the French tariff. Such bargaining, it is
argued, must give encouragement to the idea, which is the
basis of all the proposals of reciprocity and retaliation, that
the justification of a policy of free trade depends in some
degree upon the extent to which other countries are prepared
to adopt the same policy.

Considerable stress has also been laid by the opponents
of commercial treaties upon the limitations which they may
impose on freedom of action with regard to future fiscal
changes. Thus it is said that if England stipulates not to
raise the wine duties during the next ten years, there may
be serious inconvenience if during this period it became
necessary to impose fresh taxation in order to raise a larger
revenue. The justice and expediency of the principle have
now been very generally recognised, that whenever it is
necessary for us to secure increased revenue, it should be
obtained partly by direct, and partly by indirect, taxation.
Only a small minority of the electors contribute directly to
the income tax, and the policy which has in recent years
been adopted of extending exemptions from this tax, must
necessarily still further diminish the proportion. An influence in the same direction will obviously be exerted by
each fresh extension of the suffrage. If, therefore, an
augmentation of the income tax should be the source from
which additional expenditure should be wholly defrayed, a
policy which rendered this additional expenditure necessary

N

might be determined by a majority who would be able to throw the cost entirely on the shoulders of others. It is manifest that such an arrangement would not only be unjust, but would most seriously weaken all the securities for prudence and economy. It therefore may be assumed that if fresh taxation is required in order to provide increased revenue, a portion of this additional taxation will be raised from taxes on commodities. At the present time nearly the whole of our revenue from indirect taxation is obtained from the following six articles:—Beer, spirits, wine, tobacco, tea and coffee. The amount of duty imposed upon beer and spirits must evidently have some relation to the duties levied on foreign wine. Wine comes to a certain extent into competition with beer and spirits, and if wine should be more lightly taxed than beer and spirits, it would be at once objected that the foreign wine grower was favoured, and that he was protected at the expense of the home growers of barley, and the home producers of beer and spirits. The opposition which would be offered to an increase in the existing duties on beer and spirits would be undoubtedly greatly increased if we were precluded from increasing the duties on foreign wines. Hence an arrangement not to raise the wine duties during a fixed period might prevent any increase in the duties on beer and spirits, and if this were the case, the difficulties of obtaining additional revenue through an increase of indirect taxation would be greatly increased.

I have thought it desirable, before describing the beneficial results produced by the commercial treaty with France which expired in 1881, to refer to the leading objections which have been urged against the policy of commercial treaties, because if an attempt to negotiate a new treaty with France or with any other country should unfortunately fail, the feeling of irritation and disappointment which will ensue may possibly be lessened by the consideration that there are some disadvantages to set off against the benefits

conferred by these treaties.[1]   In enumerating some of these
benefits it would, as already stated, be out of place here
to attempt to estimate the advantage of these treaties
in their social and political aspects.   It is, I think, impossible to place too high a value upon establishing, through
increased commercial relations, a closer social and political
union between two such countries as France and England.
In referring, however, to the economic effect of these
treaties, I think a position of almost first prominence should
be given to the exceptionally favourable opportunities which
the negotiations afford of representing to foreign protectionists the case in favour of free trade.   If a formal
diplomatic representation were made, for instance, to the
French Government with the object of showing the injury
inflicted upon France by the maintenance of a protectionist
tariff, such a representation would in all probability be
resented as an act of undue interference.   It is, however,
abundantly shown by the negotiations which preceded the
French commercial treaty that opportunities which probably
could have been obtained in no other way were afforded of
bringing home to various classes of French traders the
losses inflicted on them by protection.   It is scarcely
necessary to remark that these opportunities were turned
to the best possible account by one who was so skilful in
argument and persuasive in reasoning as Mr. Cobden.[2]   The
various classes of traders were separately dealt with, and
to each in turn the special considerations likely to prove
most effective were addressed.   The manufacturers could
be reminded of the particular hardship inflicted upon them
by having to pay an unnecessarily high price for machinery
and coal, and the wine-growers could be readily made to see
the advantage which they would secure from having the

[1] I have thought it best to let this passage stand without alteration ;
although, as is well known, the negotiations for the renewal of the
commercial treaty with France were unsuccessful.—M. G. F.

[2] See *Life of Cobden*, by Mr. John Morley, vol. ii. pp. 293-5.

English market more freely open to them. So great an effect was exercised by these preliminary discussions that it seems extremely doubtful whether before they had taken place the French Emperor, powerful as he was at the time, would have been able to have overcome the opposition of the protectionists to the various reductions in duty which were ultimately sanctioned. There can now be little use in speculating upon what after all is an insoluble problem—whether or not these reductions in duty might have been subsequently obtained even if there had been no treaty. The supporters of the Treaty have, in view of this uncertainty, the more reason to lay stress upon the benefits conferred both upon France and England by the changes in the tariffs of the two countries which the Treaty brought about. In attempting to estimate the advantages thus conferred both upon France and England, care should be taken to avoid the mistake, to which reference has already been frequently made, of attributing the whole of the increase in the trade between the two countries to alterations in their tariffs. A portion of the increase is undoubtedly due to general commercial development; but after making full allowance for this, I believe the following brief statement of some of the facts connected with the increase of the trade between England and France in recent years will show that the Treaty has been eminently beneficial to both countries.

Between 1858, just before the negotiation of the Anglo-French Treaty, and 1882, the imports from France to England increased from 13,271,000*l*. to 39,090,000*l*., and the exports from England to France from 9,242,000*l*. to 29,758,000*l*. This great increase in the trade between the two countries shows that the French and the English obtain from each other, respectively, a large quantity of commodities which would not be obtained at all unless they were imported, or which can be imported at a cheaper rate than that for which they can be produced at home. In thus opening the

French market more freely to the English, and the English
market more freely to the French, it may no doubt have
happened that the demand for some particular article may
have been reduced in consequence of the home demand
for it being diminished. It is however important to
remember that the home and foreign demand for an
article may both be so much increased that a larger importation may be accompanied by a considerable augmentation in the home production. The value of woollen cloth
and yarn imported into France just before the Treaty in
1859 was 100,000*l*.; the value exported in the same year
was 7,000,000*l*. Thus the value of these goods exported
exceeded that imported by 6,900,000*l*. After the Treaty
had been in operation for sixteen years, the value of the
woollen cloths and yarns imported into France had increased
to no less an amount than 3,700,000*l*. But in the same
time, the value of these goods exported from France had
increased to 14,000,000*l*. It therefore appears that although
the French woollen manufacturers complain more than any
other class of traders of the injury that has been inflicted
upon them by the increased importation into France of
woollen goods from England, yet at the very time when this
increased importation had been taking place the French
woollen manufacture had developed to a remarkable extent ;
for the figures just quoted show that an increase of the
import of woollen goods of 3,600,000*l*. was accompanied
by an increase in the export of no less than 7,000,000*l*.
The amount, therefore, by which the export of woollen
goods increased, exceeded by nearly 100 per cent. the
amount by which the imports increased. Such facts as
these were persistently ignored by the French protectionists
who opposed the renewal of the Treaty. They constantly
referred to the additional quantity of manufactured articles
imported from England, as if each bale of woollen or cotton
goods sent from England to France necessarily caused
a corresponding decrease in the quantity of these goods

manufactured in France. The recent depression in the
woollen trade in France could not reasonably be attributed
to foreign importation, when there has been so great an
increase in her export of woollen manufactures. This
depression was undoubtedly brought about by causes
analogous to those which have produced depression in
England and other countries; it simply represents one of
those vicissitudes or reactions to which every trade is
liable.

The opposition offered in France to the renewal of
the Commercial Treaty with England, was assisted by
another circumstance to which it is desirable to direct
attention, because it affords an instructive example of the
influence which economic fallacies, which are generally
supposed to have been long since exploded, can still
exercise on public opinion. There is no single point on
which greater stress is laid by the opponents of the Treaty
in France than the change which has lately taken place in
the relative amount of French exports and imports. For
some years previous to 1876 the exports from France exceeded her imports. The average annual amount of this
excess was about 9,000,000*l.* In 1876 the balance was
turned in the opposite direction; for, in that year, the value
of the produce imported into France exceeded the value
of that exported by 16,000,000*l.*, and the difference has
increased, until in 1882 it amounted to 47,900,000*l.* This
change in the condition of her trade seems to have created
great alarm; the fear is widely expressed that France is
being drained of her resources, and the Commercial Treaty
is consequently the more strongly denounced because it is
considered to have been instrumental in producing this
"unfavourable balance of trade." If this excess of French
imports over exports should continue to be a permanent
feature of the trade of France in the same way as it is
of that of England, it would follow, as was shown in the
last chapter, that there has been a marked improvement

in the condition of France: that whereas formerly she was so much in debt to foreign countries that each year she had to send a considerable amount of produce abroad, in order to liquidate this indebtedness, these countries have become so much indebted to her, her wealth has in fact so much increased, that, besides receiving payment for the goods she exports, there is annually due to her a surplus amounting to many millions.

If the efforts now being made to negotiate another treaty between France and England should not be successful,[1] there are many of our own countrymen who will no doubt think that England should depart from the policy which she has been pursuing, that she should take some steps to defend her own interests, and that she should no longer continue, as is so often said, "to give everything to foreigners and get back nothing from them in return." If France, refusing to renew the Treaty, should increase the duties on English products which were reduced at the time the Treaty was first negotiated, there are those who maintain that England should in turn impose heavier duties on the articles which she imports from France. Although the undoubted right of England, under such circumstances, to increase the duties levied on French products, may be fully admitted, yet the important question to be determined is, not whether it would be justifiable, but whether it would be expedient for England to pursue such a course. The most plausible way in which it is proposed to carry out such a policy of retaliation is to impose an import duty on some article of luxury, such for instance as silk. It is urged that such a duty while encouraging a branch of home industry would inflict a deserved injury on French trade, and that no harm would be done to the English people if such an article as silk, which is chiefly purchased by the wealthy, were made somewhat dearer. If, however, such a method of attack were resorted to, an industrial

[1] See note on p. 179.

conflict would be commenced which might indefinitely
extend, and which might ultimately prove more costly to
England than a military contest. If we imposed duties on
silk with the special object of punishing the French, it is
only too probable that a spirit of pugnacity would be
aroused, and that they in their turn would retaliate by still
further increasing the duties on some English product, such,
for instance, as woollen or cotton goods. The English
cotton and woollen manufacturers would be able to put
forward an almost unanswerable claim to some protection,
for they would be able to urge, that in consequence of the
protection given to the silk trade increased impediments
were placed in the way of their obtaining access to the
French markets, while at the same time the woollen and
cotton goods of France were admitted to compete against
them on equal terms in the home market. Experience
only too surely proves, that if the principle is once sanctioned of giving one special industry protection against
foreign competition it would be impossible to withstand
the claim which would be urged by other industries to
similar protection whenever they suffered from foreign
competition.

As it thus appears that it would be inexpedient to
attempt to carry out a policy of retaliation through the
imposition of import duties, I will next proceed to inquire
whether better results would attend the proposal which has
often been made, that, in the event of France or any other
country refusing to make a commercial treaty on satisfactory
terms, we should avenge ourselves by imposing an export
duty on some article such as coal. It is said that such a
duty would not only enable us to obtain a certain amount
of revenue from foreign countries, but that nothing would
be so likely to prevent the French increasing the duties on
English goods as the knowledge that for such an increase
they would be heavily fined in having to pay a considerably higher price for all the coal they purchased from

England. At the present time only a portion of the foreign
coal used in France is imported from England. A large
quantity is obtained from Belgium, Westphalia, and other
places. It is therefore probable that the result of the duty
would be to exclude English coal almost entirely from
France. We should consequently obtain no revenue,
although a considerable amount of inconvenience might
be inflicted on France by compelling her to pay a higher
price for coal. The inconvenience which she would thus
suffer would in all probability produce an effect exactly
opposite to that which the advocates of the duty anticipate.
Instead of being induced to make concessions to England,
hostility on our part would, there is every reason to expect,
kindle increased hostility on the part of France, and a war
of tariffs, involving an incalculable loss to both countries,
would be commenced. Such an export duty however would
not only be impolitic, but it can be easily shown that even
if it were imposed its continuance would be impracticable.
As previously remarked, the recent depression fell with
exceptional severity on the coal trade. Not only were
profits and wages greatly reduced, but for a considerable
time a great number of coal mines were worked at a most
serious loss. Under such circumstances as these it would
have been impossible to have maintained a duty which,
by discouraging the export of coal, would have lessened
the demand for it, and thus have materially aggravated the
depression which had to be encountered.

Equally serious objections apply to every proposal which
has been made for the imposition of a retaliatory export
duty. Thus it has been suggested that with the object of
benefiting our manufacturers, it would be desirable to
impose an export duty on English machinery. Various
foreign countries, it is said, which restrict the importation of
our goods by protective duties, employ English machinery,
to a large extent, to manufacture articles which compete
with the products of our own industry ; and in this way we

supply the weapons of our own discomfiture. But if such a duty had been sanctioned it would, like an export duty on coal, have led to consequences which at the time of its proposal were not anticipated. Although at one time the machinery which foreign countries imported was chiefly obtained from England, yet there was nothing to warrant the conclusion that these countries must always necessarily look to England for the mechanical appliances which their own industry did not supply. We possess neither a monopoly of inventive skill, nor a monopoly of the iron, copper and other materials from which machinery is constructed. The American people are at least as inventive as ourselves, and with their inexhaustible mineral resources, there is no reason why machinery of American manufacture should not be as cheap and as good as machinery made in England. It would therefore be impossible to impose an export duty on English machinery without greatly diminishing the foreign demand for it, and we should thus inflict a very serious injury on an important branch of English trade with no other result than compelling the French, the German, and the American manufacturers either to purchase their machinery from their own countrymen, or, instead of buying it from England, to import it from some other country. The falling-off in the foreign demand may, however, be regarded as representing only a part of the harm which might be done by such a duty. With the gradual diminution of the foreign demand for English machinery, an important stimulus to enterprise and invention would cease to operate. Nothing is so likely to secure constant watchfulness to introduce every possible improvement into machinery, as the knowledge that in foreign markets we shall have to contend with the keen and active competition of other countries. It might also happen that if there were any discouragement to mechanical invention in England, foreign machinery might be more largely employed in our own industry, and thus a double disadvantage would result:

for there would be a decline not only in the foreign, but also in the home demand for English machinery.

As therefore it appears to be impossible for England, without inflicting upon herself very serious injury, to impose either import or export duties with the object of bringing pressure to bear on those countries which refuse to arrange commercial treaties with her, the question will no doubt be asked : "Can nothing be done?" It is, for instance, often said that it cannot be right for England to pursue a policy of passive indifference, and to continue to adhere strictly to the principles of free trade, when her access to foreign markets is being barred by more onerous restrictions. To the inquiry: "What ought under these circumstances to be done?"—it seems that we are irresistibly led to the answer, that, however much we may be prompted by a natural feeling of annoyance and disappointment to adopt retaliatory measures, we cannot by any possibility enter upon such a course of retaliation without greatly aggravating instead of mitigating the mischief which is done to our trade by the protectionist tariffs of other countries. It has been shown that whether it be by the imposition of protective duties on the goods which we import from these countries, or by the levying of an export duty on the products which they purchase from us, England cannot carry out a policy of retaliation without very seriously imperilling her own industrial interests. Nothing would give more encouragement to foreign protectionists than the slightest departure on our part from the principles of free trade. Such a departure would be welcomed as an omen that we had at last found it necessary to secure our industry against the evils of foreign competition. If, however, we are firmly resolved not to be drawn by any provocations, great though they may be, from a policy of commercial freedom, events will again and again occur which we may confidently anticipate will gradually bring conviction even to the staunchest supporters of protection, that the policy we thus maintain is not less just to others than beneficial to ourselves.

In order still further to strengthen our resolve not to be tempted into any departure from our present policy of free trade, it is important to bear in mind that the system of protection maintained by foreign countries, although it is highly disadvantageous to our own trade, is accompanied at least by some compensating advantages. Allusion, for instance, has been frequently made to the remarkable increase in the shipping trade of England. Not only is almost all her foreign commerce carried in her own ships, but she is gradually absorbing an increasing portion of the carrying trade of America and other countries. It has been shown that nothing more contributes to England maintaining this industrial supremacy than the burdens which are imposed on America and other countries by their protectionist tariffs. Not only with regard to shipping, but also in various other industries, protectionist countries deprive themselves of all chance of competing successfully with England in neutral markets. As an example, it may be mentioned that although other countries have the same access to the Indian markets as is possessed by England, yet it appears from the latest returns that no less than 81·45 per cent. of the imports into India come from England. But perhaps the most remarkable evidence of the supremacy which England maintains in neutral markets is afforded by the fact that, whereas the value of the English cotton yarns and manufactures exported to India and China in 1883-4 [1] was 26,600,000l., the value of American cotton goods exported to India and China was only 701,500l., and the value of the French goods only 13,600l. [2] Although we

---

[1] These figures for the year 1883-4 have been kindly furnished to me by Mr. Austin Lee of the Foreign Office.

[2] The value of the total exports of cotton yarns and manufactures from France to India and China in 1883 is returned at 464,000l., but of this only 13,600l. worth was of French manufacture.

should undoubtedly derive great advantage if the American, the French and other markets were freely open to us, yet it cannot be doubted that if these countries released their trade from its present protective fetters they would become much more formidable competitors in those neutral markets which, as the above figures show, are now so largely supplied with English goods.

As much stress has here been laid on the extent to which the protectionist cause would be strengthened in other countries if England were to sanction any departure from a policy of free trade, it may be desirable briefly to refer to the encouragement which in some quarters it is supposed is given to protection by the maintenance of the existing import duties on cotton goods in India. It is often urged by the representatives of the cotton manufacturing interest in England that this duty, being a protective tax, ought at once to be repealed by the authority of the English Parliament, and that as long as the duty is permitted to remain, a national sanction is given on the part of England to protection. The subject has lately excited an unusual amount of attention; because within the last few years many large cotton-mills have been erected in Bombay, and as some of the cotton goods imported into India are of the same kind as the goods which are manufactured in these mills, it is evident that the Bombay manufacturers enjoy protection on all the products they make which are similar in character to those imported. The economic objections which can be urged against any protective duty of course apply to this particular tax. The price not simply of those cotton goods which pay the duty is raised, but the duty causes the price of those goods which are made in India to be also raised; consequently the tax takes from the people of India an amount far exceeding that which it yields to the State. The tax therefore, like every other tax which is protective in character, must be, on economic grounds, unhesitatingly condemned. The subject, however, cannot be regarded as one involving simply economic considerations. It would scarcely be appropriate here to discuss the question in its political bearings, but it is perfectly obvious that the control which it is just and wise for the English Parliament to exercise over the taxation of any of its dependencies involves political considerations of the first importance. A more serious error can scarcely be committed than to impose taxation on a people regardless of their feelings and their sentiments. The most equitable system of taxation which it is possible to devise for one country may be altogether unsuited to other countries. Many financiers of authority who consider that the income-tax ought to be permanently maintained in England, are of opinion that in consequence of the many abuses which are inseparably associated with the collection of the income-tax in India, nothing but extreme necessity could justify its re-imposition in that country. In deciding whether the duties now imposed on cotton goods imported into India ought at once to be repealed, it is of the first importance to bear in mind the peculiar position of Indian finance. The great mass of the people of that country are so poor, and live with such extreme frugality, that with the exception of salt there is no article of general consumption which it is possible to tax; and the duty on salt has been strained to its utmost point, being one of the heaviest duties ever imposed on a first necessary of life. As therefore there remains no article of general consumption which can be taxed, it is obvious that the resources of taxation are extremely small in India; for it is scarcely necessary to remark that the taxation which is most productive is that which is levied on some article in universal use, to which therefore the whole nation has to contribute. The expenditure of India has steadily and surely increased; her revenue has advanced more slowly; frequently-recurring deficits have had to be met by borrowing; and her debt has been constantly augmented. Her financial position has been still further embarrassed by the occurrence within the last few years of no less than four famines, the cost to the Government of the last two of these famines reaching the sum of 16,000,000*l.* Under these circumstances no existing source of revenue can with prudence be surrendered ; and therefore the proposal to abolish the existing import duties on cotton goods cannot be dissociated from the question : What new taxation is to be imposed to fill the void in the revenue which the repeal of these import duties would create ? Hitherto those representatives of the English manufacturing interest who so strongly condemn these duties have not recommended any other taxation to take their place, and no new tax has been suggested which would not be either far more burdensome, or far more disliked by the people of India themselves. If the present improvement in the financial condition of India should continue, a sufficient surplus may be provided to enable these import duties to be repealed, but the permanence of the improvement ought to be insured, and other parts of the fiscal system of India, such as the salt duties, ought to be carefully reviewed, before it would be prudent to relinquish the revenue now yielded by the duties on cotton goods.[1]

Many of those who have taken a prominent part in advocating the repeal of these cotton duties have undoubtedly been prompted by a sincere dislike to England being either directly or indirectly concerned with the maintenance of any form of protection. When the immediate repeal of this protective duty is urged, it should be remembered that many English colonies maintain a system of protection far more extended and far more onerous in its character. If no attempt is made to interfere with the colonies, while it is insisted on the part of England, regardless of the wishes of the Indian people, that a particular duty which is imposed in that country shall be repealed,

---

[1] The foregoing passage was written in 1881, and the import duty on cotton goods in India was abandoned in 1882.—M. G. F.

the impression will not unnaturally be produced that India is unfairly treated, and that she is sacrificed to the interests of English manufacturers. Such a feeling no doubt already exists in India; and it has been much intensified by the manner in which the question of the repeal of these duties has been advocated in England. The subject is too often treated from the English rather than from the Indian point of view. The injury which is done to English trade by a restrictive duty is brought prominently to the foreground, and comparatively little notice is taken of the most cogent objection to be urged against this and every protective tax —that it takes from the people on whom it is imposed an amount which far exceeds that which it yields to the revenue of the State. In the appeals that are so often made that the Indian cotton duties should be abolished in order that England may consistently maintain her adherence to the principles of free trade, the mistake which may be regarded as the cardinal error of the protective. system is not unfrequently committed :—The interest of the manufacturers, as producers, is considered; the interest of the people, as consumers, is ignored.

THE END.

INDEX.

A.

B.

C.

O

www.ingramcontent.com/pod-product-compliance
Lightning Source LLC
Chambersburg PA
CBHW030123030726
47498CB00007B/2528